Table of Contents

Cover Photo for *History and Politics:*
250 Stories
https://pixabay.com/photos/people-woman-rally-protest-unite-2575608/
FOR MATURE READERS
Educate Yourself
Read Like A Wolf Eats
Be Excellent to Each Other
Books Then, Books Now, Books Forever
Do you know a language other than English? If you do, I give you permission to translate this book, copyright your translation, publish or self-publish it, and keep all the royalties for yourself. (Do give me credit, of course, for the original retelling.)

Anecdotes are usually short humorous stories. Sometimes they are thought-provoking or informative, not amusing.

This book is more interesting than it is funny. I hope it's interesting, anyway.

Dedicated to Carl Eugene Bruce and Josephine Saturday Bruce

My father, Carl Eugene Bruce, died on 24 October 2013. He used to work for Ohio Power, and at one time, his job was to shut off the electricity of people who had not paid their bills. He sometimes would find a home with an impoverished mother and some children. Instead of shutting off their electricity, he would tell the mother that she needed to pay her bill or soon her electricity would be shut off. He would write on a form that no one was home when he stopped by because if no one was home he did not have to shut off their electricity.

The best good deed that anyone ever did for my father occurred after a storm that knocked down many power lines. He and other linemen worked long hours and got wet and cold. Their feet were freezing because water got into their boots and soaked their socks. Fortunately, a kind woman gave my father and the other linemen dry socks to wear.

My mother, Josephine Saturday Bruce, died on 14 June 2003. She used to work at a store that sold clothing. One day, an impoverished mother with a baby clothed in rags walked into the store and started shoplifting in an interesting way: The mother took the rags off her baby and dressed the infant in new clothing. My mother knew that this mother could not afford to buy the clothing, but she helped the mother dress her baby and then she watched as the mother walked out of the store without paying.

***

The doing of good deeds is important. As a free person, you can choose to live your life as a good person or as a bad person. To be a good person, do good deeds. To be a bad person, do bad deeds. If you do good deeds, you will become good. If you do bad deeds, you will become bad. To become the person you want to be, act as if you already are that kind of person. Each of us chooses what kind of person we will become. To become a good person, do the things a good person does. To become a bad person, do the things a bad person does. The opportunity to take action to become the kind of person you want to be is yours.

Human beings have free will. According to the Babylonian Niddah 16b, whenever a baby is to be conceived, the Lailah (angel in charge of contraception) takes the drop of semen that will result in the conception and asks God, "Sovereign of the Universe, what is going to be the fate of this drop? Will it develop into a robust or into a weak person? An intelligent or a stupid person? A wealthy or a poor person?" The Lailah asks all these questions, but it does not ask, "Will it develop into a righteous or a wicked person?" The answer to that question lies in the decisions to be freely made by the human being that is the result of the conception.

A Buddhist monk visiting a class wrote this on the chalkboard: "EVERYONE WANTS TO SAVE THE WORLD, BUT NO ONE WANTS TO HELP MOM DO THE DISHES." The students laughed, but the monk then said, "Statistically, it's highly unlikely that any of you will ever have the opportunity to run into a burning orphanage and rescue an infant. But in the smallest gesture of kindness — a warm smile, holding the door for the person behind you, shoveling the driveway of the elderly person next door — you have committed an act of immeasurable profundity, because to each of us, our life is our universe."

In her book titled *I Have Chosen to Stay and Fight*, comedian Margaret Cho writes, "I believe that we get complimentary snack-size portions of the afterlife, and we all receive them in a different way." For Ms. Cho, many of her snack-size portions of the afterlife come in hip hop music. Other people get different snack-size portions of the afterlife, and we all must be on the lookout for them when they come our way. And perhaps doing good deeds and experiencing good deeds are snack-size portions of the afterlife.

Chapter 1: From Activism to Evil

Activism

• As an African-American child growing up in Magnolia, Mississippi, before the Civil Rights era, Jerry Butler helped his family as they grew a couple of bales of cotton each year to make a little money. When he was 13 years old, Jerry and his father took their cotton to the cotton mill to sell it. The price paid for cotton was listed in the newspaper, and Jerry knew that the amount of money the white man at the cotton mill was going to pay was much lower than it should have been. However, when Jerry spoke up, his father ordered him into their truck. On the ride back home, his father told him, "You never say anything like that in public. Never, ever, say it in public." His father was forced to let young Jerry know that raising a fuss like that with white people could be very, very dangerous. In prejudiced societies, loving parents are forced to teach their children about prejudice. As a child, Jerry also witnessed his grandmother Artise (whom he called Grand Mo Lu) integrate a restaurant in McComb, a town about six miles from Magnolia, Mississippi. Mr. Butler frequently drove his grandmother and three of her friends to the restaurant, where they ate in the colored section, and then he drove them home. However, this time his grandmother asked him to wait in the car. Very quickly, two police cars drove up because Grand Mo Lu and her elderly friends were sitting at the lunch counter — a whites-only section of the restaurant. The police officers begged Grand Mo Lu and her friends to leave because they didn't want the embarrassment of arresting four aged women. Finally, Grand Mo Lu and her friends left. Shortly afterward, three civil rights workers — white and black — were murdered in Mississippi. Later, Mr. Butler became a prominent African-American artist and writer.[1]

• Fight bad policies with wit and intelligence. For example, male legislators have introduced bills to restrict women's reproductive freedom, so female legislators have introduced bills to restrict men's reproductive freedom. Oklahoma legislators introduced a bill to make fetuses persons, so Oklahoma Democrat Constance Johnson introduced a bill to make sperm cells persons. In other words, "life begins at ejaculation" and "every sperm is sacred." Other female legislators have introduced their own bills. Illinois legislator Kelly Cassidy introduced a bill to force men who want a prescription for Viagra to watch a video on the treatment of the drug's most common side effect (persistent erections), saying, "It's not a pretty procedure to watch." Kelda Helen Roys, who was a Wisconsin legislator running for Congress, wanted men who want a prescription for Viagra to have a stress test first. State Senator Nina Turner of Ohio wanted to require men who want a prescription for Viagra to first talk to a sex therapist and get advice about "pursuing celibacy as a viable lifestyle choice." Bank of America has foreclosed on a lot of people's homes and taken their homes from them. In 2012, Occupy protestors who were part of FightBAC (Fight Bank of America) moved living-room furniture—rug, couch, coffee table, and decorative fern—into a New York City Bank of America branch.[2]

• Protesters try to speak truth to power. For example, a protestor slipped President Barack Obama this note, apparently about the Occupy Wall Street (et al.) protests, in New Hampshire November 2011: "Mr. President: Over 4000 peaceful protesters have been arrested. While banksters continue to destroy the economy with impunity. You must stop the assault on our 1st amendment rights. Your silence sends a message that police brutality is ac[ceptable]. Banks got bailed out. We got sold out." AP photographer Charlie Dharapak was on the scene and took a photograph of the note in President Obama's hand.[3]

• In 1987, director-screenwriter-producer Nora Ephron canceled an appearance at New York's LGBT Community Center because of a cold and an ear infection. Substitute speaker Larry Kramer made a speech that changed history—as a direct result of that speech, he started ACT UP, an organization of gay activists. Ms. Ephron says, "Thrilled as I am that I get credit for Larry's having started ACT UP because of that speech, I do think it's ironic that one of my major historic contributions was just staying in bed. [Laughs.] That's a little discouraging."[4]

• Sit-down protests became very popular in the Civil Rights days. In February of 1960, a protest started at a Woolworth's lunch counter in Greensboro, North Carolina. Four black students sat down and ordered food, but they weren't served. Rather than leaving, they stayed. The next day, they returned—and brought 24 friends who also sat down, ordered food, and stayed despite receiving no service. More people came to protest the next day, and by the fifth day, more than 300 blacks were protesting at the lunch counter.[5]

• Vietnam war protesters knew how to get a point across. When Luci Johnson, daughter of President Lyndon Baines Johnson, got married, protesters were outside the wedding area carrying two open coffins and this sign: "Wedding Rice for Starving Vietnamese—Deposit Here." Some protesters once threw confetti on Pat Nixon, the wife of President Richard Nixon. The confetti were printed with the message, "If this was napalm, you would be dead."[6]

AIDS

• In 1991, Eileen Mitzman's daughter died of AIDS. Following the death, Ms. Mitzman became active in Mother's Voice and began to educate people, including politicians, about AIDS. In one of her first trips to Washington, D.C., she spoke about AIDS to Senator Ted Stevens of Alaska. When he stated that there was no problem with AIDS in Alaska, she said, "Well, there will be. If there isn't right now, then there will be. My daughter lost her life to AIDS at the age of twenty-six. Not her house to a hurricane or an earthquake, but her life." Senator Stevens replied, "Well, we have people in Alaska who are dying of cancer," and he walked out of the room.[7]

• The first National Coming Out Day for homosexuals was held on October 11, 1988. This day was chosen because October 11 was the date on which the Names Project Memorial Quilt was first shown, and because it is the birthday of Eleanor Roosevelt, a champion of human rights for all. The first gay pride march was held in New York City on June 28, 1970. After parading up Sixth Avenue, several thousand gay men and lesbians held a "gay-in" in Central Park, where they celebrated, held hands, and kissed.[8]

Art

• The Sforza family once gave Leonardo da Vinci the commission of creating a huge bronze statue of a horse. He set to work, and in 1493, he created a 23-foot-high clay model of the proposed statue. The model was impressive, and it was displayed during the wedding celebrations of Bianca Marie Sforza. Unfortunately, in 1499, before the bronze statue could be completed, French troops invaded Milan, and they used the clay model for target practice. For centuries, the plans for the horse were thought to be lost. Fortunately, in 1965, two lost da Vinci manuscripts were discovered on a shelf in the National Library of Madrid. They include da Vinci's notes on and drawings of the bronze statue of the horse.[9]

• The village of Kake on Kupreanof Island in the southeastern part of Alaska is the location of one of the largest totem poles in existence. The totem pole was made by the Native Americans known as the Tlingit and is over 132 feet tall. The Tlingit created the totem pole in 1971 so it could be displayed at an international exhibition in Japan. Because of the totem pole's great height, it had to be cut in half so it could be shipped to Japan for the exhibition. Afterward, the totem pole was brought back to Kake and displayed.[10]

• The entrance hall to Thomas Jefferson's home, Monticello, looked like a museum. In it were displayed many items Meriwether Lewis and William Clark had brought back from their journey to the USAmerican West, including a buffalo hide on which was artwork depicting a battle between the Mandan and the Dakota Native American tribes. Thomas Jefferson was a clever man. His bookcases at Monticello were made from the crates that he had shipped his books in.[11]

• Sometimes, people are more prudish than they should be. Some of the figures Michelangelo Buonarroti painted on the ceiling of the Sistine Chapel are nudes. Later, other artists painted clothing on the figures to hide their nudity.[12]

Astronauts

• Being weightless in space affects astronauts in ways you may not expect. For one thing, the astronauts' blood isn't pulled down by gravity to their legs and feet, so the astronauts' faces get puffy. For another, because gravity isn't pulling on the astronauts' backbones, the astronauts get taller—sometimes as much as one inch taller. Readjusting to gravity makes landing back on Earth difficult. In fact, scientists have developed special pants for astronauts. The pants have tubes that can be inflated to put pressure on the astronauts' legs so their blood doesn't rush to their legs when they re-enter the Earth's atmosphere and begin to be affected by gravity. If too much of their blood rushes to the astronauts' legs, the astronauts could lose consciousness due to lack of blood in the brain. Here's some trivia: When astronauts Sally Ride and Steven Hawley married in July 1982, two ministers performed the ceremony. One was the Reverend Dr. Bernard Hawley, Steven's father. The other was the Reverend Karen Scott, Sally's sister.[13]

• On his 16th birthday, Neil Armstrong, who became the first person on the moon, received his student pilot's license—before he received his driver's license. When the *Eagle* landed on the moon on July 20, 1969, astronaut Neil Armstrong was at the controls. He had seen that the landing area was rocky and dangerous, so he took over from the computer and searched for a safe place to land. Fortunately, he managed to land safely with only 30 seconds of fuel left. Back on earth, one of the NASA control men stated, "I think he's the greatest pilot in the whole world."[14]

• John Glenn passed all the tests that were required to become one of the United States' first seven astronauts. Some of the tests were grueling. For example, he spent two hours in a 135-degree heat chamber. He spent time with his feet in ice water. And to see how he would handle being alone in space, he spent three hours alone in a dark room. On February 20, 1962, Mr. Glenn became the first American to orbit Earth.[15]

Astronomers

• The telescope was invented by Hans Lippershey, a Dutch lens grinder who regarded it as a toy. However, other people, including Galileo Galilei, realized the new invention's great importance. Galileo created a better and more sophisticated version of the telescope, which he then showed to the senate of Venice in 1609. The senators were greatly impressed with the telescope's potential use in the military, and they rewarded Galileo by doubling his salary at the University of Padua and by making his job there permanent. Galileo then began to use the telescope to explore the sky. He discovered that the Moon has mountains, that Venus has phases like the Moon, that the Milky Way is made up of great numbers of stars, that the constellation known as the Pleiades consists of many more stars than the six that are visible, and that Jupiter has moons orbiting it. Such discoveries made Galileo one of the greatest astronomers ever.[16]

• Benjamin Banneker, an African-American astronomer and mathematician, was born on November 9, 1731, and he lived in Baltimore County, Maryland. On January 4, 1763, when Benjamin Banneker was 32 years old, he bought the first book he ever owned, a secondhand Bible, from a woman named Honora Buchanan. Mr. Banneker accomplished most of his significant educational attainments in his later years. He first used a telescope when he was 57. He helped survey the site of Washington, D.C., when he was 59. The first of six straight annual almanacs for which he made the astronomical calculations was published when he was 60. For it, he calculated such things as sunrises and sunsets, moonrises and moonsets, the positions of the planets, and eclipses.[17]

• Maria Mitchell was an early American astronomer. On October 1, 1847, at 10:30 p.m., as she searched the sky with her telescope, as she habitually did, she discovered a fuzzy object that had not been there previously. Ms. Mitchell had become the first person to discover a comet with the aid of a telescope. Because of this accomplishment, the King of Denmark awarded her a medal.[18]

• American astronomer Percival Lowell believed that there was an additional planet beyond the orbit of Neptune. Before he died in 1916, he undertook a systematic search for the planet but never found it. Later, the search was continued, and on March 13, 1930, the planet Pluto was discovered. The symbol for the planet is PL, in honor of Percival Lowell. In 2006, by the International Astronomical Union (IAU) reclassified Pluto as a dwarf planet.[19]

Biology and Biologists

• Here are three Charles Darwin stories: 1) As a young man, Charles Darwin was free with his father's money—he used to hire choirboys to come to his rooms and sing for him. 2) As a young man, he studied medicine, thinking he would become a physician. However, as part of his training, he witnessed an operation performed on a child—in the days before anesthesia was invented—and he rushed out of the operating room and never returned. 3) Late in his life, Charles Darwin was ill and sometimes unable to hold up heavy books and read them. To solve that problem, he often had heavy books divided into parts light enough for him to hold.[20]

Celebrities

• Following the War of Independence, General George Washington became a celebrity. Visitors came to his home, Mount Vernon, to see where he lived, and they sometimes knocked on his door in hopes of meeting him. When he became President, he and his wife sometimes held "open houses," so that anyone who wanted to stop by could meet him. When George Washington died, his will stated that all his slaves would be freed when his wife Martha died.[21]

• Ronald Reagan was once asked to autograph a poster that showed himself and his co-star in *Bedtime for Bonzo*: a chimp. He did autograph the poster, and he added this note: "I'm the one with the watch."[22]

Chemistry and Chemists

• Here are three stories about chemists: 1) Antoni Van Leeuwenhoek made the best microscopes of his time, and he was the first person to see bacteria, red blood cells, and sperm cells. After Mr. Van Leeuwenhoek died, he left 26 of his microscopes to the group of scientists known as the Royal Society of London. Before his death, he had guarded his microscopes carefully, seldom giving one away and even declining to let other scientists look at his best microscopes. 2) Because of his government job, Antoine Lavoisier, the founder of modern chemistry, did most of his experiments between 6 and 8 a.m. and between 7 and 10 p.m. In addition, one day a week he was free to perform experiments all day. His wife called this one day a week his "day of happiness." 3) The French Revolution degenerated into a Reign of Terror, and in September of 1792, mobs gave 1,400 political prisoners trials that lasted one minute each and then executed them with guillotines. The death toll did not stop there, as more innocent people were killed. In 1794, Antoine Lavoisier, the founder of modern chemistry and a true French patriot, died at a guillotine.[23]

Children

• Madeleine K. Albright, the 64th Secretary of State of the United States, wanted the approval of her parents when she was young. At first, she earned that approval by doing such things as earning points for a team she was on at school. But then she started to invent fictional exploits to get more praise — praise that she did not deserve.

Eventually, she said that she had won the Egyptian Cup at school — but no Egyptian Cup existed. Her parents wanted to see the Egyptian Cup, but of course that was impossible, so young Madeleine made up more lies, including lies that she was being mistreated at school: "They even make me sit on needles!" Her protective mother went to the school — and discovered that young Madeleine was lying. Afterward, whenever Madeleine said something that seemed different from the truth, her parents would say, "Egyptian Cup."[24]

• President Theodore Roosevelt said, "I can do one of two things. I can be President of the United States, or I can control Alice. I cannot possibly do both." Alice was his daughter, age 17 when he became President. She was a wild child. She had a green pet snake that she named Emily Spinach, and when the President forbade her to smoke in the White House, she climbed up on the roof and smoked there. After marrying Nicholas Longworth, she hosted many dinner parties, at which she seated next to each other sworn enemies. At age 90, she astonished guests at a Washington D.C. dinner party by sitting in the full lotus position and placing a boa constrictor across her shoulders. Alice knew herself. She said, "I just perform." She added, "I give a good show."[25]

• Penn Jillette of Penn and Teller fame really dislikes the whole princess thing that little girls—such as his daughter when she was little—get into. He told her, "Lady Di was an evil wh*re! Why did anybody in America like her? She's a symbol of everything bad! Susan B. Anthony—women's rights, atheist, abolitionist ... everything Susan B. Anthony did was right! Dress up like her! Dress up like Madame Curie! There are female *heroes* you can dress up as! Don't do the *princess* thing!" Penn's sister-in-law listened to Penn's diatribe and then said to him, "You know, Penn, I don't think it's meant that seriously. I think it has more to do with playing dress-up and the nice pretty gowns. I don't think she's thinking all that much about keeping down the proletariat." [26]

• Godfrey Hounsfield enjoyed working with mechanical things. At age 13, he made a record player out of spare parts. His curiosity led him to develop the CT Scanner, which is capable of taking 3-D pictures of a living brain. In 1979, Mr. Hounsfield won the Nobel Prize for Physiology or Medicine.[27]

Christmas

• Not every memorable Christmas is happy. In 1942, Lieutenant General Garrison H. Davidson was in Casablanca, which was filled with many refugees, many of whom had very little. He wanted to make Christmas merrier for some of the refugees, so he proposed to other servicemen that they do just that. They went to a clergyman and asked him to find the four most destitute families in each of four parishes. They then gathered food, clothing, and toys for each family. On Christmas Eve, teams—each consisting of an officer and three enlisted men—set out to visit the families. Of course, Lieutenant General Garrison H. Davidson was in one group. The families knew that they were coming and had cleaned their homes. In each home were women and children—no men. The team gave their gifts to each family, and Lieutenant General Garrison H. Davidson said, "The women kissed our hands and wept. The children hugged us. Then came the pictures—'my daddy before he was killed'—'my husband before he went to war'—'my son when I last saw him.'" Lieutenant General Garrison H. Davidson and the other Good Samaritans did manage to relieve a little poverty, but they saw much more poverty—more than they could bear. Many impoverished people had heard about the gifts, and they had assembled. As the group of Good Samaritans left, they were surrounded by impoverished people, all of whom were women and children. Lieutenant General Garrison H. Davidson said, "Women with dirty children in their arms tugged at our sleeves with pitiable pleas. 'Food for my baby, too.' Urchins grasped at our trousers. 'Candy? Toys for me?'" The teams of Good Samaritans had started the day with elation, but ended the day with depression, and the depression far outweighed the elation. General Garrison H. Davidson said, "The next three Christmases overseas, we considered playing Santa Claus to some foreign children again. Never were we man enough to subject ourselves to a repetition of the depression of that memorable first Christmas overseas in Casablanca." Note to politicians by David Bruce: If you want to help the world, avoid starting unjust wars. Also, work for a strong economy even if that means going against your political party's orthodoxy. Raise the minimum wage. Note to multi-millionaire and billionaire business-men and -women: Pay your employees well. Note to everyone by David Bruce: Good charities are worth supporting.[28]

• Q: A creche is a representation of the Christmas story. It shows Joseph, Mary, the baby Jesus in a manger, some animals, and sometimes shepherds and the three wise men bearing gifts. Who created the first Christmas creche? A: In the year 1223, St. Francis of Assisi created the first creche in the grotto of Greccio in Italy.[29]

• When he was a boy, Isaac Newton, who was born on Christmas Day, 1642, carved his name in his wooden desk. The part of the desk bearing his name still exists today.[30]

Civil Rights

• Rosa Parks lived with her grandparents and her mother as she was growing up. Her grandfather had been badly abused when he was a slave, and he was determined never to undergo that kind of treatment again. During the 1920s, the Ku Klux Klan terrorized families throughout the South, including Pine Level, Alabama. Ms. Parks remembered staying up with her grandfather one night—he was holding a shotgun in case the KKK showed up. Fortunately, they never did. Of course, the Montgomery, Alabama, bus boycott started when black seamstress Rosa Parks declined to give her seat to a white person while riding on the Cleveland Avenue bus line. Today, Cleveland Avenue has been renamed Rosa Parks Boulevard.[31]

Computers

• Here are three stories related to computers: 1) One of Microsoft founder Bill Gates' most expensive purchases was a notebook that he paid $30.8 million for—the notebook originally belonged to Leonardo da Vinci, and in it he had drawn plans for such inventions as submarines and steam engines. Originally, the notebook had been named the Codex Leicester, after the Earl of Leicester, who had purchased it in 1717. For 263 years, the notebook was called the Codex Leicester, but after Armand Hammer bought it, it became known as the Codex Hammer. Mr. Gates declined to call it the Codex Gates, and he instead gave it again its old name of Codex Leicester. 2) Microsoft founder Bill Gates' mother was a remarkable woman. Mary Gates served on the boards of several big organizations, including United Way and First Interstate Bancorp. When she was a schoolgirl, her friends called her "Giggles." 3) The name "Microsoft" comes from two other words: "microcomputer" and "software." The name "Big Blue" comes from the blue suits its executives wear. The name "Macintosh" comes from the name of Apple Computer co-founder Steve Jobs' favorite apple.[32]

• So many Ph.D.s worked at Intel Corporation that co-founder Robert Noyce finally told the workers not to use the title "Doctor" when calling researchers over the intercom—the computer company was starting to sound like a hospital![33]

Controversies

• At various times, people have thought that harmless things were dangerous. Frederick the Great, the King of Prussia from 1740-1786, was against the drinking of coffee, preferring instead that his soldiers drink health-giving beer. (Some people even told women that drinking coffee would make them sterile.) In the mid-1800s, a new dance craze that was considered by many to be highly scandalous swept through Europe—it was the waltz.[34]

Critics

• At one time opera houses were infested by claques—groups of people who would either applaud or hiss opera singers. Some of the claques were run for money. If the opera singer would pay them, they would applaud the opera singer. If the opera singer would not pay them, they would hiss the singer off the stage. One leader of a claque tried to blackmail Maggie Teyte before her appearance with the Philadelphia Opera Company. He named his terms: "One hundred and fifty dollars for three curtain calls, after each act; for each additional curtain call, $25 extra, and $50 for shouting at the end of the performance, 'Maggie Teyte.'" Ms. Teyte then asked what would happen if she did not pay the money. The leader of the claque replied, "I shall have 50 men at the opera house tonight ... they will hiss you off the stage." At this point in the conversation, Ms. Teyte's husband, accompanied by a police officer and a reporter, came into the room. They had been listening from an adjoining room, and the police officer arrested the leader of the claque.[35]

• George Canning (1770-1827) was blunt. Once a clergyman asked how Mr. Canning had liked his sermon. Mr. Canning said, "You were brief." The clergyman responded, "Yes, you know I avoid being tedious." Mr. Canning replied, "But you were tedious." Another blunt man, Antoine de Rivarol (1753-1801), once said about a poem that was only two lines long: "Very nice, though there are dull stretches." [36]

Danger

• This story appears in a biography of Courtney Love titled *Courtney Love: Queen of Noise*: Drug addiction is harsh, and often the addict values the drug more than anything else. At a party, an addict went inside a bathroom and locked the door. He did not come out. Eventually, the other people at the party kicked in the door and found that the addict in the bathroom had died of an overdose while shooting up—the needle was still in his arm. One of the dead man's friends, who was also an addict, took the needle out of the dead man's arm, looked at it, and said, "Hey—still a hit left."[37]

• Roger Ebert had a friend named McHugh, who frequented O'Rourke's, where he saw someone who had a pistol stuck in his belt. He asked, "What are you carrying that for?" The guy replied, "I live in a dangerous neighborhood." McHugh told him, "It would be a lot safer if you moved."[38]

Death

• A study of history reveals fascinating stories about the legendary ways that some people have died. 1) Nicocreon, the tyrant of Cyprus, executed the philosopher and skeptic Anaxarchus by placing him into a mortar big enough to hold a human being and ordering him pulverized by iron pestles. But the philosopher denied that he was his body and shouted as he died, "Pound, pound the pouch containing Anaxarchus—you do not pound Anaxarchus." 2) Pythagoras stayed away from beans, and when an assassin pursued him, he refused to save his life by crossing a bean field. The assassin caught him and cut his throat. 3) Dionysius, the tyrant of Syracuse, tortured Timycha, Pythagoras' assistant, to find out why the philosopher so disliked beans. She would not tell him, preferring instead to bite off her own tongue and spit it at him, knowing that he would then have her killed. 4) The ancient Egyptians believed in facing up to one's own death. They hosted skeletons at parties, and told guests, "Drink and be merry, for when you are dead you will be like this."[39]

• In 1692, the Salem Witch Trials resulted in the hanging of 19 people, mostly women. In addition, a man named Giles Corey was "pressed to death." Mr. Corey had refused to testify at his trial because he knew that if he testified and was found guilty of being a witch, all his property would legally be seized by the British government. Since no accused person had been found innocent in the trials, he felt that he would definitely be found guilty. However, if he did not testify in court, he could not be found guilty according to the laws of the time, although persons who refused to testify suffered "a punishment hard and severe." Mr. Corey was 80 years old, but his jailors decided to torture him to make him confess. They made him lie down on his back, and then they put a board over him and loaded heavy flat stones on the board. Mr. Corey was a man of courage, and he still declined to testify. Eventually, so much weight was placed on him that his rib cage caved in. (Fortunately, the use of torture in modern USAmerican trials is illegal. The Eighth Amendment of the United States Constitution states, "Excessive bail shall not be required, nor excessive fines imposed, nor cruel and unusual punishments inflicted.")[40]

• In 1425, Joan of Arc, who was only 13 years old, first began to hear what she called the voices of Christian saints and heavenly angels telling her that she must come to the aid of the dauphin, who was the oldest son of the King of France and therefore the rightful heir to the throne. In 1429, she began to aid the dauphin and was instrumental in having him crowned Charles VII, King of France. During her early military campaigns against the English invaders, Joan of Arc achieved amazing success as she relieved the siege of the city of Orléans. Following this success, she and the French army stormed Jargeau. There she told the Duke of Alençon to stop standing at a certain spot; otherwise, a piece of artillery in Jargeau would kill him. The Duke of Alençon followed her advice and moved. Shortly afterward, another man stood there and was killed.[41]

• Weber and Fields (Joseph Weber and Lew Fields) were an early vaudeville comedy team. Mr. Weber's family had immigrated to the United States from Poland. They almost took a ship from Liverpool, but missed it. That ship sank, and everyone on board drowned. When they did take a ship to the United States, the youngest child—who was only an infant—died. They did not want the infant to be buried at sea in shark-infested waters, so Mrs. Weber kept the dead infant with her and pretended to be feeding it. Once they arrived in America, the first thing they did was to have a funeral.[42]

• Crawford Goldsby, aka Cherokee Bill, was an African-American outlaw in the Wild West who murdered as many as 36 men. He was so feared that a town council passed a law mandating that whenever he came to town, no one was to do anything to bother him. At his public execution on March 17, 1896, a guard asked the 20-year-old outlaw if he had any last words. Cherokee Bill replied, "No. I came here to die—not to make a speech."[43]

• While John Barrymore was on his deathbed in the hospital, his friend Gene Fowler telephoned Diana, Mr. Barrymore's daughter, who said, "I can't make it—I have an important appointment." Mr. Fowler replied, "So does your father," and hung up.[44]

• Kate Moore, a USAmerican widow in the days of King Edward VII, was known as a social climber who enjoyed dining with great people. When she died, it was said of her, "Ah! This will be a great night for Kate! No doubt she will be dining with God."[45]

Dinosaur Hunters

• During the late 1800s, O.C. March and William Cope engaged in a race to discover the best and most impressive dinosaur fossils. This competition probably resulted in greater efforts from both men than either would have made otherwise, but the "bone wars" had some bad effects for the study of dinosaurs. For example, one of Mr. Marsh's bone hunters, William Reed, once found several dinosaur fossils. He carried off the best ones for Mr. Marsh to look at, but he smashed the remaining fossils to make sure that Mr. Cope would find nothing of value left at the site.[46]

• While searching for dinosaur fossils in the Gobi Desert, Roy Chapman Andrews had little success at first. However, one day he had trouble pitching his tent and thought he had hit a rock. The "rock" turned out to be a dinosaur fossil. He kept trying to pitch his tent, and he kept discovering dinosaur fossils. Eventually, he pitched his tent—after discovering over 50 dinosaur bones.[47]

Education

• President Ronald Reagan asked George Schultz to write a speech for him, and when the speech was over, he read it and said, "That's perfect." He hesitated and then added, "Of course, if I was doing it, I wouldn't do it this way." He then edited the speech for four minutes and gave it to Mr. Schultz, who noticed among other marks the word "story." President Reagan then said, "You've written this speech to be printed in *The New York Times* and as a State Department bulletin, but when I give a speech, I give it to people. Where you're trying to make a point that's maybe a little abstract, tell a story so that people can put themselves into it. Then they get it." What was Mr. Schultz' reaction? He thought, "This guy is an instinctive teacher. He wants the people on the other end of the television camera to learn something."[48]

• As a youth, Noble Prize-winning physicist Niels Bohr cared about accuracy in his schoolwork. When he was 11 years old, he was given an art assignment: to draw a house that had a garden with a picket fence. Before Niels drew this scene, he carefully counted the pickets in the picket fence. In high school, he was already reading current scientific journals, and so he knew when his high-school textbooks contained inaccurate passages. When a fellow student asked him what he would do if the teachers asked in an exam questions about some of these inaccurate passages, Niels replied, "Tell them, of course, how things really are."[49]

• Noble Prize-winning physicist Niels Bohr was born in Copenhagen and of course grew up speaking Danish. When he decided to learn English, he got a copy of Charles Dickens' *Pickwick Papers* and read it, looking up each word he did not already know in a red dictionary even when he could guess its meaning from its context. He used his red dictionary for the rest of his life.[50]

• When opera singer Leo Slezak was in the Austrian army, he taught other soldiers bugle calls by whistling them and having the other men imitate his whistles. Once he saw a man scribbling in a notebook and thought his efforts to teach were being ignored. However, when he looked in the man's notebook, he found that the man was writing down the bugle call: "Tadaradatataratatada!"[51]

Evil

• As Speaker of the House of Representatives in the late 19th century, Tom "Czar" Reed, a Republican, used his power to push through Republican legislation. In the days before votes were counted electronically, he used to read a bill, ask for a vote orally, then say whether the bill had passed or not based on his own inclination, not on the votes of the elected representatives of the people. Once, he said "the ayes have it" on a bill he wanted passed. A colleague rose and said, "Mr. Speaker, I was listening very carefully, and I am sure the ayes did not have it on that last vote." Czar Reed told the Representative, "When I am in the chair, the ayes always have it," and then he read the next bill and used his own inclination to pass or not pass that bill.[52]

• In Cleveland, Dave Paige ran against Captain A.S. McClure in a campaign to be elected to Congress. Mr. Paige knew that Captain McClure was popular with the Republican steelworkers in the district, so he realized that the election would be difficult to win. Therefore, he found a man who resembled Captain McClure and sent him to give a speech to the steelworkers. After the speech, the "Captain" ordered two beers, which he and the master of ceremonies drank in front of the steelworkers. The very next night, Mr. Paige gave a speech before the steelworkers. In his speech, he made the same promises that the "Captain" had made, and after the speech, he bought a round of drinks for everyone. Mr. Paige won the election.[53]

Chapter 2: From Fathers to Law

Fathers

• When political cartoonist Herblock's father was courting his mother, he was not above using his position as a journalist to impress her. Once, he took her to a variety show, but they arrived late and missed the first number; this disappointed her. He talked to the management and said that he was a critic who needed to see the *entire* show. The management believed him, and the performers doing the second number were taken off the stage so that the first number could be performed again. Journalists had a different code of ethics back then. Herblock's father was assigned to cover a speech by a politician. Because of bad weather, he did not make it to the site of the speech, so he wrote a speech and submitted it to his newspaper, saying that the politician had made the speech. Unfortunately, the politician also did not make it to the site where he was supposed to give the speech. Fortunately, the politician read "his" speech in the newspaper and liked it.[54]

• Jackie Bouvier's father loved her and was proud of her and wanted her to do well in school. He wrote very nice letters to her, including this one: "Do hard work, don't waste your time, but take advantage of all opportunities to get ahead, whether it be in your studies or in little daily lessons that confront you each day. You know I'm proud of you. Always keep me that way, never let me down, and always remember in your own heart that I will never let you down. I miss you and love you a great deal." Of course, Jackie later became Mrs. John F. Kennedy.[55]

Fires

• Wiring was a major problem in the old Metropolitan Opera in New York, as wires ran this way and that. The wiring was also dangerous. Frederick Williams once laid down his flute on the stage apron. Suddenly there was a flash, and in its wake, a melted flute. On August 27, 1892, the Metropolitan Opera burned down because of measures to save money. The New York architect of the Met had used many fire safety measures in its design, including a sprinkler system, fireproof construction, an iron stage curtain, and metal supports for the stage. However, to save money, many of these measures were abandoned, with the result that a worker's cigarette placed too near some flammable scenery destroyed the building.[56]

• The Great Fire of London destroyed 87 churches and over 13,000 homes in its four days and four nights of burning. The night it started, Sept. 1, 1666, Samuel Pepys' maid woke him up, but after looking out the window, he went back to bed. In 17th century London, fires were common. The fire spread because the Lord Mayor did not want to create a fire break by pulling down houses. Some good resulted from the fire—it stopped the plague by killing the rats that were believed to be spreading it.[57]

Food

• Back when Ted Kennedy was running against Eddie McCormack for the Democratic nomination for the United States Senate, William "Billy" Bulger was a young state representative whom Ted wanted to endorse him. Ted invited Billy and a lot of other Boston state legislators to lunch at Locke-Ober, a very expensive restaurant in Boston. Billy had heard about the house specialty, lobster Savannah, and so he decided to attend the luncheon. Billy later remembered that "everybody ordered soup (30 cents) or tuna fish salad ($1.85). No one ordered both. When it came to me, I ordered lobster Savannah." The lobster Savannah cost $10—a huge amount at the time. All of the politicians endorsed Ted, except Billy, who remembered, "When it came to me, I said—between bites of succulent lobster—'I can't be with you, Ted. The McCormacks are my neighbors.'" Ted's campaign manager still wanted his endorsement, so he asked, "Could you at least stop eating for a minute so we can talk with you?" But Ted joked, "I don't know whether we should try to persuade him. I don't think we can afford to feed him."[58]

• During the Russian Revolution, the ballet schools carried on. The pointe shoes were of poor quality, the schools were freezing cold, and there was little to eat, but ballet was still taught. During a production of *Sleeping Beauty*, Madame Smirnova was lying down, waiting to be kissed by the Prince. She was wearing her fur coat, because the theater she was performing in was so cold it was if she were lying down in the cold street outside the theater. Also, during the Russian Revolution, food was scarce. The mother of young ballerina Illaria Obidenna Ladré got hold of some butter and used the butter as payment to Ms. Vaganova, a ballet teacher, for private lessons for Illaria.[59]

• The Methodist pioneer circuit riders were known for their healthy eating habits. On one occasion, a group of circuit riders, including Jesse Lee (who weighed 259 pounds) arrived at a farm during harvest time. Neighbors were working in the fields to help bring in the harvest, and the farmers' family had worked hard preparing a huge meal to feed the neighbors who were helping them. Unfortunately, the circuit riders ate, and ate, and ate, and when the harvest was finished and the neighbors arrived to be fed, very little was left. One of the neighbors said this blessing: "Oh Lord, look down on us poor sinners, for the Methodist preachers have come and et up our dinners. Amen." [60]

• After a failed revolution in Panama, ballerina Margot Fonteyn's husband, Tito Arias, took refuge with the Brazilian ambassador. As they were eating, a disturbance was heard outside. The ambassador had the disturbance investigated, and when Tito asked what the noise was, the ambassador told him, "They are asking for your head." Tito calmly replied, "Tell them it is busy—eating."[61]

• Senator Jay Rockefeller once spoke at a $500-a-plate dinner after winning a close Senate race—in which he spent a fortune of his own money: "Some of you might feel cheated, paying $500 for a lousy chicken dinner, but just think about me—I spent $10 million to be here."[62]

• Benjamin Franklin tried to be a vegetarian, but after seeing several codfish cut open and noting that they had smaller fish inside them, he thought, "If you eat one another, I don't see why we mayn't eat you." He then sat down and enjoyed a fish dinner.[63]

Free Speech

• Mort Sahl got his satiric comedy act from newspapers. The head of Fox Cable News, Roger Ailes, once saw him read a newspaper, then perform his act six hours later with 40 minutes of new satiric observations that he had created from his reading of the newspaper. After the Supreme Court elected George W. Bush President with a 5-4 vote in 2000, satirist Mort Sahl said, "The American people have spoken—all five of them." Comedian Dick Gregory was sometimes introduced as "the Negro Mort Sahl." He would reply, "In the Congo they call Mort Sahl 'the white Dick Gregory.'" [64]

• Freedom of speech was a right not recognized by the Nazis. In 1941, Marion van Binsbergen visited a friend's apartment in her native Holland. Ms. van Binsbergen didn't know it, but the students in the apartment listened to radio broadcasts by the Allies and even made recordings of them for distribution. The Nazis raided the apartment while she was there and arrested both her and the students. For her "offense," she spent the next seven months in prison. After getting out of prison, she became a rescuer of Jews.[65]

• Barbara Kingsolver and some friends went to a shopping mall and started distributing some literature about some aspects of the Gulf War that were not pleasant. However, she and her friends were asked to leave the mall. They protested that another group at the mall was handing out Gulf War literature that stated such things as "We kick butt." The mall officials replied that the other group was performing a public service, but Ms. Kingsolver and her friends were doing something political.[66]

• Richard Strauss was a musical genius, but he was also the leading musical figure among the Nazis. For that reason, many people did not want his music to be played in the United States during and after World War II. One person who disagreed was conductor Bruno Walter, who stated, "I dislike Strauss as a person, and I abhor everything for which he stood. But Strauss is a genius, and some of his works are masterpieces. I cannot, in all honesty, boycott masterpieces because I detest their composer."[67]

Games

• In 1996, when Vice President Al Gore spoke at the graduation ceremony of MIT students, the graduation students played "Al Gore Buzzword Bingo." The students had bingo cards that lacked numbers, but which did have buzzwords such as "information superhighway," "Infobahn," "paradigm," and "empower." Every time Mr. Gore said one of the buzzwords, the students would mark out that square. The students who got five buzzwords in a row were instructed (the instructions were printed on the card) not to shout "BINGO" — "which would be rude and potentially upset the men with wires in their ears" — but to hold up the card so that Mr. Gore could see it.[68]

• Dorothy Parker used to play a game called Botticelli. In it, someone thinks of a famous person or character—for example, Twain—and then gives the other players the initial of the character. The others would then ask questions, such as "Do you write comic short stories for *The New Yorker*?" The person would then either know who the questioner was asking about and reply, "No, I am not Thurber," or the questioner would have to identify Thurber. One day, when the letter was "H," Ms. Parker asked, "Do you chase men for business and for pleasure?" The askee didn't know the answer, so Ms. Parker revealed it: "J. Edgar Hoover."[69]

Gays and Lesbians

• A homophobe once said to lesbian comedian Judy Carter, "Homosexuals are already covered under the Constitution just like the rest of us. What they want are special rights. We oppose special rights for homosexuals." She replied, "If *special* means the right to get and keep a job based on merit, equal access to housing, renting a hotel room and being served in a restaurant ... if *special* means the right to have and raise children without the state seizing them, and the right to walk down a street and not get attacked because of who you are and whom you love ... then you're right: I want the same special rights of all American citizens. And it looks as if you want the very special right to discriminate against those you hate. We call that 'special righteousness.'" By the way, one of Judy's lovers brought her to meet her parents, but asked her to not act gay. Ms. Carter asks, "What exactly does that mean? As if I am going to eat dinner and then hump the hostess!"[70]

• When gay Congressman Barney Frank came out of the closet in 1987, Tip O'Neill told him, "It's too bad, Barney. You would have made a great Speaker of the House." By the way, in New York City is a printing firm run by lesbians that advertises, "We're Here, We're Queer, and We Do Quality Printing."[71]

• The first public figure in the United States to publicly support gay rights was feminist Emma Goldman, who supported Oscar Wilde during his legal trials. As early as 1910, Ms. Goldman was speaking publicly in support of gay rights.[72]

Golf

• Professional golfer Sam Snead once played Vice President Dan Quayle, who won $10 from him. Following the 18th hole, Mr. Snead paid up, but all he had was a $20 bill. Mr. Quayle didn't have change, so he went to get change. While he was gone, a crowd gathered around Mr. Snead. When Mr. Quayle returned and handed $10 to Mr. Snead, a woman asked Mr. Snead, "You mean you won money from the Vice President?" Mr. Snead smiled and replied, "What does it look like?" [73]

• Professional golfer Sam Snead once had an audience with the Pope at the Vatican and his friend Fred Corcoran suggested that he take his putter along so the Pope could bless it. However, before the audience with the Pope they met a monsignor who complained about his poor golf game and poor putting—his golf scores were in the 100s! Hearing that, Mr. Snead put away his putter, saying, "If you're that close to the Pope and you can't putt, he ain't gonna be able to do anything for me."[74]

• The upper class seems to have always loved golf: 1) John Smith "Sodger" Mcintyre often caddied for Prime Minister J.A. Balfour. After a bad shot, Mr. Balfour would tell Sodger, "If I always got what I wanted, I would never play golf." 2) Mary, Queen of Scots, was such a fanatical golfer that in 1567 she was seen golfing a few days after her husband, Lord Darnley, was murdered. 3) In the mid-1800s, golfers at the Royal and Ancient Golf Club at St. Andrews in Scotland sometimes ran into problems. Women used to do laundry and lay it out on the fairway to dry and bleach, and sometimes a golf ball would land on the clothing. 4) The Latin motto of the Royal and Ancient Golf Club at St. Andrews in Scotland is *"Dum spiro, spero,"* or, in English, "While I breathe, I hope."[75]

Good Behavior

• Good behavior is important: 1) Joe Garagiola knew better than to tell "funny" stories about physical handicaps during a speech. He once listened to a pitcher tell a story about a person with a harelip during a speech. The pitcher got lots of laughs, but after the speech, several children came up to get the pitcher's autograph. One boy, who had a harelip, said, "I can't help this, but I still like you." Mr. Garagiola says, "I remember hoping that his class would rub off on the player. I'm not sure it did, but that night, it was the youngster who was the real champion." 2) Some religious people don't ask God to take sides at sporting events. Father George Tribou once prayed, "Grant to the referees, the linesmen, and the umpires sharpness of vision and fairness of judgment that they may see from the sides with the same clarity with which You will be watching from above."[76]

• The Native Americans were frugal, something considered a virtue in many societies. The Tlingit, Native Americans of Alaska and other parts of North America, used all parts of the animals they caught. They ate the meat of a deer, used its sinews to sew, made moccasins from its hide, and so forth. Also, they believed that things came to a person for a reason. A Tlingit woman who found a piece of copper would find a way to use it—for example, to scrape an animal hide and make it soft. [77]

Good Deeds

• When Hanci Hollander was in Auschwitz during the Holocaust, she was fortunate enough to find a friendly Hungarian guard who showed her a photograph of his granddaughter and who pointed out that he was not a guard in Auschwitz by choice. Near the end of 1944, Dr. Josef Mengele inspected the Jews, selecting those who looked the weakest for extermination. Hanci was selected, and she and other prisoners were put in a truck to be taken away to be killed. The driver of the truck was the friendly Hungarian guard, who told the prisoners that at times he would drive slowly so that any prisoner who wished could jump off the truck and escape. However, he requested that if any prisoner should be recaptured that the prisoner not tell what he had done. Hanci was the only one who jumped off the truck and escaped—the others were too deadened by hardship to save their own lives. Many troubles still lay ahead for Hanci, but she survived the Holocaust and moved to the United States, Americanized her name by changing it to Gloria, married Karl Lyon, raised a family, and started speaking publicly about her Holocaust experience after seeing a pamphlet with this title: "A Zionist Hoax: The Holocaust Never Happened." Annuska, her sister, also survived Auschwitz, although she could have been killed upon arrival. Annuska, who was only 12, was placed in a group of old people and young children. Hanci thought that that was good news because the old people would look after Annuska. However, Annuska made her way back to Hanci after a Nazi soldier was mean to her. She climbed in the back of a wagon when no one was looking, and the wagon carried her back to Hanci. Later, Hanci discovered that the Nazis had killed all the old people and the young children.[78]

• Cheeky Watson was a highly rated white soccer player in apartheid-era South Africa. In 1976, he began to help coach a new team of black soccer players despite the legally mandated segregation that existed then. Seeing the conditions in which the black team practiced and played, Mr. Watson grew furious. The white teams had fully lighted soccer fields. The black team he helped coach had to practice in the lights of five automobiles despite the existence of fully lit soccer fields nearby. Mr. Watson asked for permission for the black players to use the fully lit fields at his soccer club, but the white soccer teams, including his own team, turned down his request. He quit the soccer club. He coached the black soccer team after 5 p.m. because all the players worked in factories and could not practice or play any earlier. Because of this, he was found guilty of breaking a law that forbade a white person from being present in a black township after 5 p.m. Mr. Watson gave up much in his stand against apartheid, including a chance to be a member of the South African national soccer team, but he does not regret it. He says, "I can sleep at night because I have a clear conscience."[79]

• Lillian D. Wald was a major figure in establishing public-health nursing in the United States; she also was a believer of the power of the arts to improve people's lives. Among her many accomplishments was persuading New York's Metropolitan Museum of Art to be open on Sundays so that the working class—who often worked on Saturdays before the advent of the 40-hour week—could enjoy it. She also convinced the city to establish many parks and playgrounds for underprivileged children.[80]

Hasidism

• Here are some Hasidic stories: 1) Rabbi Nachman of Bratslav wanted to see the Holy Land of Israel. In 1798, at age 26, he decided to make the journey. His middle daughter pleaded with him not to go, asking who would look after his family while he was away. He replied, "Go to your parents-in-law; your elder sister will become a servant. People will have pity on your younger sister. Your mother will become a cook. I will sell the household goods to provide the means for the journey." He made the journey, stayed in Israel for a while, and always spoke with longing of Israel after he returned home. 2) Isaac Meir Rothenburg, also known as the Hiddushe Harim, once visited Rabbi Moses Eliakim Briah, who kissed him. But the Hiddushe Harim told him, "I do not want a rabbi who embraces but one who chastises and rebukes." 3) Hiddushe Harim greatly respected Rabbi Mendel of Kotzk. In the middle of winter, in the days when such journeys were dangerous, he took his grandchildren to Kotzk to see Rabbi Mendel, justifying the journey by saying, "It is all worthwhile in order that they should behold a true Jew." 4) Rabbi Shalom Rokeach had a wife who was eager that he study and who regarded study as service due to the Creator. When she woke him each day, she said, "Arise, Shalom, to the service of the Creator."[81]

Heroes

• Heroes don't always appear when they are needed. Anita Schorr survived the Holocaust. In 1939, when she was 10 years old, the Nazis entered her native country: Czechoslovakia. Ms. Schorr said, "My childhood ended right there." Things changed gradually. Curfews were imposed. Dress codes were created and enforced. Jewish children were segregated and could not go to parks or a swimming pool or school. She remembers the lack of food: "You went to sleep hungry. Day after day you fought the hunger. There was disease, scarlet fever, hepatitis, jaundice." She said that she kept thinking two thoughts: 1) "This is not humane. This is not what one person does to another," and 2) "Nobody in the free world said, 'This cannot be done to another human being.'"

Ms. Schorr added, "Nobody stood out and said 'No!'" In 1941, she and her family were told to pack up and enter a concentration camp. She remembers, "Everything was at night. At night it's more scary. You are more nervous. Everything was unknown. Everything was planned for you, and you knew it was not good." At the concentration camp, the men were separated from the women and children. Ms. Schorr went into a barracks. She said, "We were shoved onto bunk beds — they were more like shelves. Suddenly you were lying down next to a total stranger." From 1941 to 1945 she lived in three different concentration camps. She said that while she was imprisoned, "I didn't lose the desire to live. I did lose faith in mankind. That took time to rebuild. I went between thinking I survived because God saved me, versus asking where God was and how could He watch to see such injustice." In 1945, Allied soldiers liberated the prisoners in the camp. Ms. Schorr gives advice while she speaks about her experience in the Holocaust: "You cannot stand there and let it happen. Remember my words. We all have to step in and be a hero every day."[82]

• The United States at its best believes in justice and giving a fair trial even to a killer caught red-handed. Roosevelt Grier is a big man—a retired NFL player—and he campaigned for Robert Kennedy when Mr. Kennedy was running for President of the United States. When Mr. Kennedy was assassinated, Mr. Grier was present. He had been assigned to guard Ethel Kennedy, who was six months pregnant. When he heard shots, he made sure that Mrs. Kennedy was safe, and then he rushed toward the sound of the shots. He grabbed a man who was waving a gun in the air, and he took the gun away from the man. He held on to the man. Many people wanted to hurt—even kill—that man, but Mr. Grier protected him by covering him with his body, even though he was crying because he could see Mr. Kennedy's bleeding body. Because of Mr. Grier, the world was spared an additional act of senseless violence.[83]

Holocaust

• Harry Spiro is a survivor of the Holocaust, and he has experienced things that we hope never to suffer. He remembers, "When someone fell, you felt lucky you were next to him. The dead always had something useful." The conditions in the Nazi-ran camps were unimaginable. Mr. Spiro remembers, "I didn't think about survival. I thought: another day, another problem." For example, "In Buchenwald there were three bunks on top of each other and at the beginning you would go to the bottom bunk. You learned that was a mistake. The people on the top bunk couldn't get out of bed in the night so they would urinate on you." Near the end of the war, he was forced to go on a death march from Rehmsdorf labor camp to Theresienstadt in Czechoslovakia. The name "death march" is accurate because only 300 of the 3,000 people who were forced to undergo the death march made it to the end alive. Mr. Spiro remembers, "The majority were killed because they couldn't walk. If you fell over, the SS man would very calmly say, 'Get up, otherwise I'll shoot you.' And then if you repeated it, they would shoot you." At one point, bombs fell, and young Harry dived into a ditch in the field for safety. In the ditch, he saw something in the field he could eat: turnips, aka white beetroots. He put one in his pocket, but the turnip was not unnoticed. Another boy saw it and requested a piece to eat. At first, Harry said, "No," but the boy said, "'If you don't, I will tell everyone what you've got, and they will crush you to death." Harry gave him a piece, and another piece, and another piece, and finally told the boy, "Ask again and I'll give you a knife [in the gut], not beetroot." After the war, the boys became business partners. The other boy's name was Harry Balsom, and the two Harrys started and ran a firm of tailors.[84]

• During the Holocaust, Jews were sometimes able to escape being sent to concentration camps by hiding in the woods—and sometimes in caves. In the Ukraine, several Jews (mainly three families—the Stermers, the Dodyks, and the Kurzes) hid for months at a time in two separate caves. Some of the Jews left at night to get food and supplies, but some stayed underground the entire time. Esther Stermer and her family were among these Jews hiding from the Germans. She said to her oldest son, "We are not going to the ghetto. We are not going to go to the slaughterhouse. Go into the forest, find a hole, any hole, any place." They did find a hole that led to a cave. Esther and most of the Jews survived, although they had to move from one cave to another after the Germans found them. Her strong spirit and the loyalty of her family and of the other Jewish families kept them alive in the worst times possible. After the Russian army arrived (the Russians and the USAmericans were among the Allies fighting the Germans), they left the cave. Pepkale Dodyk, who was one of the children in the cave, had forgotten about the sun, and because it was so bright, she asked her mother to put out the light. They entered a Displaced Persons camp. Eventually, the Stermers came to the United States, where Esther wrote a book in Yiddish about their survival. In 1973, the book, *We Fight to Survive*, was privately printed in English. In this book, she wrote, "The world had turned animal—or worse. Every day conditions became worse. Death stalked each step ... But we were not surrendering to this fate. Our family in particular would not let the Germans have their way easily. We had vigor, ingenuity, and determination. Above all our family would stand together."[85]

• In Lvov, Ukraine, Luncia Gamzer hid in the home of a Gentile woman named Mrs. Szczygiel and her parents hid in the home of a Gentile man named Mr. Ojak during the Holocaust, but hiding Jews was dangerous. A Gentile who was found to be hiding Jews could end up dead. This led to much tension among many of the Gentiles who were hiding Jews. Sometimes, the Gentiles had their own children whom they worried about. What would happen to the children if the parents were killed by the Nazis? Mrs. Szczygiel and her family worried about this because she was hiding Luncia. Even after her family decided—after narrowly being caught—that hiding Luncia was too dangerous, Mrs. Szczygiel kept on hiding her from the Nazis—and this time, from her husband and children. Unfortunately, one of her daughters discovered that Luncia was still being hidden in their home. Therefore, Mrs. Szczygiel took Luncia to the man who was hiding her parents and told him, "We can't keep her any longer. You have to take her." Mr. Ojak was completely surprised—he had no idea that he would be asked to hide another Jew. He hesitated a long time, and then he said, "She can stay. If I'm caught, it's the same death for me whether I'm hiding two Jews or three." Luncia had a joyous reunion with her parents. After surviving the Holocaust, the Gamzers came to live in the United States, where Luncia changed her name to Ruth and married a Holocaust survivor named Jack Gruener.[86]

• Among the rescuers of Jews during the Holocaust was Swedish diplomat Raoul Wallenberg, who personally saved at least 20,000 Jews and who saved tens of thousands more Jews by preventing the bombing of Jewish ghettos in Budapest, Hungary. At times, he even had Aryan-looking Jews dress up in Nazi uniforms, descend upon a detention center in Hungary, and take away hundreds of Jews destined for the death camps. Even as a child, he was sensitive to cruelty. Young Raoul hated hunting because he hated the killing of animals. Therefore, one night before a hunt was scheduled, he sneaked into his neighbor's kennels and let the hunting dogs loose. Also, even as a child, he exhibited great courage. During a thunderstorm, the other children hid inside a house, but he ran outside, shouting, "Let's see God's fireworks." Frequently, because he was a rescuer of Jews, his life was in danger; however, he said, "My life is one life, but this is a matter of saving thousands of lives." Eventually, he was captured by the Russians and never seen again, apparently dying in a Russian prison.[87]

• Eddie Weinstein nearly died in Treblinka during the Holocaust. He and some other prisoners were ordered to strip off their clothes, and he knew that that was a prelude to death. Fortunately, he noticed some prisoners digging a trench to serve as a latrine, and he made his way there. Challenged by a guard, he said that he had been ordered to help dig the trench. Also fortunately, one of his friends was helping to dig the ditch. Seeing Eddie, and realizing that Eddie had a reason to be there, the friend called to him, "Eddie, get over here and back to work!" Eddie was lucky—he soon managed to escape from Treblinka by hiding in a cattle car. Eddie survived the Holocaust and wrote a book about his experiences titled *17 Days in Treblinka*.[88]

Hunting

• In the days of the buffalo hunters, the professionals were tormented by the antics of the amateurs, who didn't know what they were doing and made a mess of things for everybody. Eventually, the professional hunters gave the amateur hunters all the meat they wanted so that the amateurs wouldn't scare all the buffalo away. Today we see people gathering aluminum cans to make a few dollars. In the old days, people in West Texas used to gather buffalo bones—left over from when the buffalo were slaughtered in huge numbers for their hides—and sell them back East for use as fertilizer.[89]

• Amateur hunters caused enormous waste in West Texas, as recounted by Texas journalist/historian Don Hampton Biggers. Once, an enormous number of wild turkeys could be found there. However, amateur hunters would surround a tree where a few thousand turkeys roosted at night, and in the dark, they would shoot dozens of shots each at the tree. In the morning, dead turkeys would be lying on the ground and wounded turkeys would be fluttering in the tree. The amateur hunters would pick up a few dead turkeys, then let the others go to waste. The wild turkey population was further devastated by the bringing in of hogs to West Texas because the hogs developed a taste for turkey eggs.[90]

Illnesses and Injuries

• Ballerina Margot Fonteyn's Uncle Arnulfo was shot in a political battle in Panama. He was a doctor, and he knew that the resulting operation on his throat would be a delicate one that could result in mistakenly cut vocal cords. Therefore, he insisted on going through the operation without an anesthetic so that he could talk throughout, thus ensuring that the operating doctor would see his vibrating vocal cords. [91]

• Antonio López de Santa Anna lost much of his left leg below the knee while fighting the French in Mexico. A man of great ego, he held a funeral for his leg. Unfortunately, he was often unpopular with the people of Mexico—despite being the President of Mexico five times—and in December of 1844, some Mexican citizens dug up his leg and burned and pulverized it.[92]

• Joy Behar is both a fervent comedian and a fervent Democrat. When she had surgery, her surgeon told her that he had voted for George W. Bush. She made him promise to NEVER again vote Republican. She says, "I wanted to stop the operation, but it was too late. I was already anesthetized and starting to go under."[93]

Insults

• After being called a "two-faced man" by his political opponent Stephen Douglas, Abraham Lincoln said, "I leave it to my audience—if I had another face to wear, do you think I would wear this one?" By the way, here are some quotations by President Lincoln, 1) "The better part of one's life consists of his friendships." 2) "I don't think much of a man who is not wiser today than he was yesterday." 3) "Better to remain silent and be thought a fool than to speak out and remove all doubt." 4) "It is said that an Eastern monarch once charged his wise men to invent an aphorism to be ever in view, and which should be true and appropriate in all times and situations. They presented him the words, 'And this, too, shall pass away.'"[94]

• Abraham Lincoln was frequently critical of George McClellan, a notoriously unaggressive and indecisive Union general. Once President Lincoln visited Union headquarters when General McClellan was absent. He found some soldiers working nearby to build a privy for the general. President Lincoln asked, "Is it a one-holer or a two-holer?" The soldiers answered, "It's a one-holer." Later, out of the earshot of the soldiers, President Lincoln told his aide, "Thank God it's a one-holer, for it were a two-holer, before McClellan could make up his mind which to use, he would beshit himself."[95]

Language

• Country comedian Jerry Clower was a Christian first. Some people wonder why he hadn't received the gift of speaking in tongues, but he said that although he did not doubt the power of the Holy Spirit to give him any gift, he had noticed that sometimes being able to speak in tongues had bad results. For example, when some people received that gift, they were advised not to take medicine any more. Mr. Clower says, "Some of them ended up in the insane asylum because the medicine was taken from them. I wouldn't do any criticizing or point a finger at anybody, but I'll tell you one thing—anytime something happens to hurt the cause of Christ, it's no kind of gift from God. You write that down. I've seen happy Christian couples in the church, then one of them would get this gift of speaking in tongues and it'd end up in unhappiness ... at home, and in the church. God is not the father of any kind of unhappiness."[96]

• Here are two Curie stories: 1) Marie Curie was Polish, and some of her servants were Polish, although she lived most of her adult life in France. During World War I, Marie sent her daughters to live for a time in L'Arcouest, a fishing village in Brittany in northwest France. Some of the villagers accused the daughters of being German, because they spoke a foreign language to their servants. That language, of course, was Polish. To keep the villagers from making unfounded assumptions, one of Marie's daughters, Irène, began to teach the servants French. 2) Marie and Pierre Curie first discovered radium and first isolated it. It was very useful in treating certain kinds of cancers, and it was very expensive. To build the Curie Institute, the price was 800,000 gold francs. The price of one gram of radium was 50,000 gold francs fewer. [97]

• In 1808, Isabella, a slave, was put up for sale in New York. No one bid for her, so the auctioneer threw in a flock of sheep, and John Nealy bought both Isabella and the flock of sheep for $100. Later, Isabella earned her freedom and then became famous after taking a new name: Sojourner Truth. Sometime in or around 1797, she had been born the slave of Colonel Johannes Hardenbergh in Hurley, New York. He taught his slaves only Dutch, not English, because he felt that he could control his slaves if they could not communicate with anyone outside his own property.[98]

• When George W. Bush was elected President, he stated that he could not believe the *enormity* of his being elected. President-Elect Bush did not know that *enormity* means excessive wickedness, outrage, and monstrous evil.[99]

Law

• In 1430, during an assault on Compiègne, Joan of Arc fell off her horse. Armor at that time consisted of heavy plates of inflexible metal. Because of the weight and inflexibility of the armor, she was unable to remount her horse and so was captured by her enemies, the Burgundians, who handed her over to the English army then occupying part of France. The English then turned her over to some members of the Inquisition who supported their side in the war. These biased individuals found her guilty of several crimes, including heresy, and in 1431, they turned her over to the English again, who burned her at the stake. In 1456, a retrial was held, and the name of Joan of Arc was completely cleared of any wrongdoing. In 1920, Joan of Arc was made a saint by the Catholic Church.[100]

• At the Salem Witch Trials in 1692, which resulted in the deaths of 20 people, girls who suffered from fits supplied evidence against supposed witches. One of the afflicted girls screamed at the trial and said that the specter of Sarah Good had stabbed her, and she showed the judges a piece of knife that she said had been used to hurt her. However, a man testified that during the previous day he had broken a knife and he had seen the girl pick up one of its pieces. He produced the broken knife, and the piece of knife the girl had produced was found to fit the broken part exactly. The girl was reprimanded—lightly—and Sarah Good was hanged. (Fortunately, reforms have made the use of spectral evidence in modern USAmerican trials illegal.)[101]

- A law professor taught his class the tricks of the trade: "When you're fighting a case, if you have the facts on your side, hammer them into the jury. If you have the law on your side, hammer it into the judge. But if you have neither the facts nor the law on your side, hammer the table."[102]

Chapter 3: From Letters to Prayer

Letters

• To bedevil racist politicians, H.L. Mencken once invented a fictitious society whose purpose was to advance the cause of black people. He had stationery made up with the logo of "The American Institute of Arts and Letters (Colored), the Rev. Hannibal S. Jackson, A.B., A.M., Ph.D., LL.D., DD., Chancellor and Financial Secretary." Mr. Mencken used this stationery to send letters to racist politicians telling them that they had been elected to the institute's membership and inviting them to the institute's inaugural banquet.[103]

• To make a point, Benjamin Franklin once wrote a letter to a London newspaper, in which he argued that the United States should send rattlesnakes to England because the British send their convicts to the United States.[104]

• Ohio Senator Stephen M. Young once received a letter that was short and to the point: "Do something." Senator Young's reply was also short and to the point: "I did. I read your letter."[105]

Mathematicians

• The ancient Greek mathematician and scientist Erastosthenes (c. 276-c. 194 B.C.E.) successfully calculated the circumference of the Earth, among other accomplishments. However, there is evidence that he was not respected by some of his intellectual peers. Because he was interested in so many intellectual pursuits, other scholars called him "Beta," the name of the second letter of the Greek alphabet, implying that they thought he was a jack of all trades and master of none, and therefore did not rate being called "Alpha," the name of the first letter of the Greek alphabet. In addition, because of his wide interests, they called him "Pentathlos," after the Olympic Games events called the pentathlon, in which the athlete competes in many different athletic endeavors.[106]

• Archimedes designed war machines for the city of Syracuse, and he died when the city was taken after a long siege. He was busy working a geometry problem during the attack, and when an enemy soldier found him, Archimedes asked if he could finish the problem before the soldier killed him. The soldier did not oblige; instead, he killed the famous scientist immediately.[107]

Media

• Chicago newspaper are good sources of legendary stories: 1) Chicago reporter Harry Romanoff was a good man on the telephone, and he impersonated many notabilities to get information. After a Chicago police officer was killed, newspapers wanted a photograph of the police officer, but his family was secluded and would not admit into the house any of the Chicago reporters, including Jack McPhaul, who worked at the *Examiner* with Mr. Romanoff. However, the door of the house opened, and the widow asked, "Where's the *Examiner* man?" Mr. McPhaul came forward, and the widow let him inside, led him to the telephone, and said, "The captain wants to talk to you." Not surprisingly to Mr. McPhaul, Mr. Romanoff was on the telephone. Mr. Romanoff said, "Don't let on. She thinks I'm the district captain. I've told her the *Examiner* is the police department's best friend. She'll give you his picture. Hustle it down here." Mr. McPhaul left the house with a photograph of the slain police officer, much to the disgust and envy of the other rival reporters. 2) War sells newspapers. Wilbur Storey bought the Chicago *Times* for $13,000 just three months before the Civil War began. He regarded the Civil War simply as a way to sell newspapers. He even told his war correspondents, "Telegraph fully all news and when there is no news send rumors." William Randolph Hearst also used war to sell newspapers. Before the Spanish-American war, artist Frederic Remington was a Hearst newspaper employee stationed in Havana, where all was quiet. He telegraphed Mr. Hearst asking to return home. Mr. Hearst replied, "Please remain. You furnish the pictures, and I'll furnish the war." 3) After a tornado wrecked some towns in Illinois, the *Chicago Herald-Examiner* gathered supplies and sent them to the cities by train. A big banner on the side of the train's cars said, "*Herald-Examiner* Relief Train." The relief train was news, and the Chicago *Tribune* sent a photographer, but when the early edition of the *Tribune* was published, a *Tribune* artist had changed the banners so that they read "Chicago Relief Train" to avoid giving a rival newspaper positive publicity. Frank Carson, city editor of the *Herald-Examiner*, tore the photo from the page, wrote on it, marked it "Must Correct," and then sent one of his copy boys, who had formerly been a *Tribune* copy boy, to the *Tribune*, where he tossed it on a copy cutter's desk, knowing that it would find its way to a linotype operator. The *Tribune* printed 25,000 copies of the photo with the banners reading "*Herald-Examiner* Relief Train." Then it reverted to the "Chicago Relief Train" banners. When a copy of the *Tribune* with the "*Herald-Examiner* Relief Train" photo arrived at the *Herald-Examiner*, Mr. Carson danced in celebration.[108]

• During the Joseph McCarthy era, Clifford Odets defended his cooperation with the House UnAmerican Activities Committee by saying that there were some things he wanted to say to the committee, and the only way he could say them was to cooperate. Alfred Crown, a movie producer and a friend of an actor whose career was destroyed by the blacklist, replied, "You could have taken an ad. I would have paid." [109]

• In 1976, Dan Quayle first ran for the U.S. Senate. Once he ran into a man who said that he was going to vote for him—until he found out that Mr. Quayle was a lawyer. Mr. Quayle pointed out that although he had a degree in law, he didn't practice law. Interested, the man asked, "What do you do?" Mr. Quayle replied, "I publish a newspaper"—and the man said, "Heck, that's worse."[110]

Mishaps

• Rich people have problems, too. Lee Radziwell, who was the sister of Jackie Kennedy Onassis, and Truman Capote were friends.

Once, after her husband, Stas, gave her a new sable coat, Lee visited Truman, and they went to the movies, with Lee leaving her new fur coat behind. When they returned from the movies, they saw Charlie, Truman's pet bulldog, lying on part of the coat. Around him were the shreds of the rest of the coat. Truman thought it was funny and laughed. Lee says, "For him, everything provided a pretext to laugh." When Jackie was still married to John F. Kennedy, she and Caroline, her four-year-old daughter (and Secret Service agents), visited the Radziwells in Italy. They and other people visited a house near Naples. Lots of people in Italy kept a shotgun on a table in the living room. Such was the case here. A guest picked up the shotgun and fired it, not realizing that it was loaded. Of course, the Secret Service came running. And when Lee was a very young lady, she felt her underwear fall around her ankles at a fancy event. Fortunately, she was wearing a very long skirt, so no one knew what had happened. She survived the evening by hopping and clasping her ankles.[111]

• George Haven Putnam was Executive of the Copyright League from 1886-1891 and worked for the passage of bills to protect the copyrights of authors. Often he testified before Congress, sometimes taking along an author to buttress his arguments about the importance of a bill to provide copyright protection. Once he took along Mark Twain, but as soon as the members of Congress saw Mr. Twain, they immediately cried out for a story. For the next hour, Mr. Twain told anecdotes. Finally, the members of Congress had to leave, although no testifying had been done about the bill before Congress. After that experience, Mr. Putnam was careful not to take Mr. Twain along when he went to Congress.[112]

• The most applause Lotte Goslar ever received was in Chicago, where she performed in a benefit for Czechoslovakian compatriots. At the end of her first dance, thunderous applause arose, and she made at least 15 curtain calls. At the end of her last curtain call, she went to the front of the stage and saw that all the members of the audience had their backs to her. They weren't applauding her at all—they were applauding Czech President-in-exile Eduard Benes, who had entered the theater just as her dance ended.[113]

• Ruth St. Denis played the role of Miriam, Moses' sister, at the Greek Theatre at the University of California. The theatre bore a marble plaque: "The Greek Theatre, a Gift of William Randolph Hearst." One night, she erred in one of her lines. Instead of saying, "And I shall make visible the heart's corruption," she said, "And I shall make visible the Hearst corruption." The audience was amused by the error.[114]

• Federal judge Leon Yankwich sat on the bench in Los Angeles. Once, a Phoenix lawyer started to read a long technical document. A few minutes later, he looked up, noticed that the judge was not sitting at the bench, and whispered to his partner, "Where did that little SOB go?" Judge Yankwich had climbed down from the bench to look over the lawyer's shoulder as he read the document, so he said from behind the lawyer, "Here I am."[115]

• Juliette Gordon Low, founder of the Girls Scouts in 1912, did not sweat the small stuff. She once suggested that a Girl Scout meeting be held in Hawaii because it was "central" to both Central and South America. When someone pointed out Hawaii's actual location, she replied, "Maybe I meant Haiti. Why should we bother about minor details?"[116]

• Benjamin Franklin didn't know much about French oratory, so at a social function he watched his friend, Madame de Bouffleurs, and he applauded whenever she seemed to say something that pleased her audience. Afterward, Mr. Franklin's grandson told him, "You were applauding whenever they praised you—and much louder than anybody else."[117]

Money

• Syndicated columnist Marc Dion (the Mike Royko of today) is good with money, normally saving almost 30 percent of his salary. He does the very good thing of saving right away, instead of waiting until the end of the month to save, because at the end of the month no money is left over to save. Basically, he gets his paycheck, and then he pays his bills, puts money into savings, and sticks the rest of his money in his pocket. As long as he has money in his pocket, he spends. When the money in his pocket runs out, he stops spending until his next paycheck. I get the feeling that he eats roast beef just after he gets paid and sometimes he eats bologna just before he gets paid. He says, "I can read my bankbook like some people read a novel. In fact, when one of my banks stopped using bankbooks, I moved my account. I like to see myself saving money." He also remembers the example of his father, and he emulates him. When Marc had knee surgery and had to live for a while on disability pay (60 percent of his normal salary), he stopped drinking. He remembers the uncertain economic times his family went through for a while when he was a small child. He says, "My dad bounced from job to job for a while. When he lost a job, he would take his last drink on the day he got laid off and his next drink when he got a new job. 'I'm not buying a drink with my unemployment check,' he used to say. 'What do I look like, a bum?'"[118]

• African-American Mary Fields, aka Stagecoach Mary, ran away from slavery in Tennessee and moved first to Ohio and then to Montana. She was six feet tall and could outfight nearly every man. One day, a man who owed her two dollars for laundry walked into a local saloon where Ms. Fields was drinking—the mayor of Cascade, Montana, had given her special permission to drink with men. Ms. Fields saw the man and yelled at him, "Hey, you. Come here. When are you going to pay me for that laundry?" The man ran away, but Ms. Fields ran after him and pinned him to the ground, saying, "If you don't pay me the $2 you owe me for that laundry, you won't get up." The man paid the $2, and Ms. Fields went back to the saloon and announced, "His laundry bill is paid."[119]

• Gore Vidal tells this story about John "Jack" F. Kennedy: John's father was Joseph Kennedy, a very wealthy man who spent large amounts of money getting John elected to public offices, including the Presidency. After John was elected President in 1960, Joe took all nine of his children, including John, to Palm Beach, where he told them, "All you read about the Kennedy fortune is untrue. It's non-existent. We've spent so much getting Jack elected, and not one of you is living within your income." Joe then turned to John and asked, "Mr. President, what's the solution?" John answered, "The solution is simple. You all gotta work harder."[120]

Music

• Here are some blues stories: 1) Few people's lives were as tough as Billie Holiday's. When she was a child, she went to sleep next to her great-grandmother. When she woke up, she discovered that her great-grandmother had died and her great-grandmother's cold, lifeless arm was around her neck. To recover from that shock, young Billie spent a month in a hospital. 2) Blues guitarist Walter "Furry" Lewis invented what is known as the "Mississippi Bottle Neck" method of playing guitar. He broke the neck off a bottle, heated it in a fire to smooth the place where it had broken, put it on the little finger of his left hand, and slid it along the guitar strings as he played. 3) African-American blues singer Tommy McClennan got into trouble at a party in Chicago because he used the word "n*gger" in a song although his friend and fellow blues singer Big Bill Broonzy warned him that up north blacks didn't like the word even though southern blacks such as Tommy used it. After Tommy sang the word "n*gger," fighting broke out and Tommy had to escape by jumping out a window. 4) The great blues singer Bessie Smith was singing professionally at age nine in Cincinnati, Ohio, at the Ivory Theater. With her very first weekly paycheck of $8, she bought herself some roller skates, but her mother spanked her because her family needed to use the money to buy food.[121]

• Here are some music anecdotes: 1) African-American diva Reri Grist insisted on adequate rehearsals before singing. In Vienna, she was once told that there wasn't time to hold a stage rehearsal for *Figaro*. She replied, "Then I don't sing." Time was found to hold a stage rehearsal. 2) Ethel Roosevelt was a force for integration. When the Southern Conference on Human Welfare was held in Birmingham, Alabama, she shocked people by sitting beside African-American educator Mary McLeod Bethune. 3) When George Gershwin died, he stipulated that his opera *Porgy and Bess* could not be performed by any but a black cast. This stipulation is usually observed in USAmerica, but it is not always observed in Europe. 4) Lillian Evanti (1890-1967) had an Italian-sounding name. Actually, she was an African-American singer who created the name by combining her real last name, Evans, with the last name of her husband, Roy Tibbs.[122]

• Tourists may visit Ludwig van Beethoven's birthplace at Bonn and see his piano, which is roped off to protect it. One tourist ran past the rope, sat down at the piano, and played the opening notes of Beethoven's Fifth Symphony. As a security guard escorted her away from the piano, she said, "I suppose that everybody tries to play something on Beethoven's piano." The security guard replied, "When the great pianist Ignacy Paderewski was here, he said that he was not worthy to touch it."[123]

• Mayor Fiorello La Guardia, mayor of New York City, loved music. Once he was asked to conduct the band of the New York Fire Department at Carnegie Hall. Learning that the director of the hall planned to make the concert a special occasion, La Guardia told him, "Please, no fuss. Just treat me the way you would treat Toscanini."[124]

• Mrs. John Jacob Astor was an influential society lady in New York in the early 20th century, and others imitated whatever she did. Because she habitually arrived late at the opera, many others also arrived late—with the result that the first half of each opera was played to half-empty houses.[125]

• The King of Holland once attended a piano recital by Clara Schumann; afterward, he met her husband, the famous composer Robert Schumann, and asked, "Are you musical, too?"[126]

Names

• Thurgood Marshall's name at birth was Thoroughgood. He changed the spelling when he was in the second grade because he got tired of having such a long first name. As a lawyer, he helped get rid of segregated schools by arguing the court case *Brown v. Board of Education of Topeka*. Later, he became a Supreme Court justice.[127]

• Mary Poole, the great-great-great-great grandmother of author Alice Walker, was a slave who was forced to walk from Virginia to Georgia while holding a child on each hip. To honor this ancestor, Ms. Walker vowed not to give up her name when she married.[128]

Native Americans

• Before the Pueblo, a Native American people in the southwestern United States, dig clay from the earth, they often pray to Clay-Old-Woman and tell her that they will treat the clay and the pottery they make from it with respect. Many Pueblo believe that Clay-Old-Woman is the spirit of clay, and if they treat the clay with respect, Clay-Old-Woman will help them to create beautiful things with it. In addition, she will live within the clay and protect the pottery made from it. One item the Pueblo make from clay is a two-spouted water jar that is used in wedding ceremonies. During the wedding, the pot is filled with water, and then the family of the groom and the family of the bride drink from different spouts. Afterward, the pot is broken to bring good luck for the wedded couple.[129]

• In the southwestern corner of Colorado lies a place called Mesa Verde, where Native Americans lived long ago. A staple food of these Native Americans was corn, which they ground with stones to make into cornmeal, from which they made cornbread. Scientists believe that this process of making cornmeal was bad for the Native Americans' teeth, because grit from the stones got into the cornmeal. When chewing the cornbread, the Native Americans would also chew the grit, thus wearing down their teeth. The Native Americans who lived at Mesa Verde in Colorado sometimes used turkey feathers to make blankets to keep themselves warm during winter weather.[130]

• The Onondagas are a free Native American people in New York, and they are part of the Iroquois Confederacy. They have their own nation, and when an Onondaga travels, he or she uses an Iroquois passport, not a United States passport.[131]

Nobel Prize

• Here are some Nelson Mandela stories: 1) The first black President of South Africa, Nelson Mandela, was named at birth Rolihlahla Mandela. In the language of his people, the Xhosa, "Rolihlahla" meant "pulling the branch of a tree." Later, when he began attending school, his teacher, Miss Mdingane, gave him the name "Nelson," possibly because Europeans found it difficult to pronounce African names. Later, when he was 16, he was given yet another name after being circumcised in a ritual that marked his coming into adulthood. His circumcision name was "Dalibunga," which can be translated as "the founder of the rulers of the Transkei." (The Transkei is a region in South Africa that is the Xhosa people's traditional homeland.) 2) Nelson Mandela, a member of the Xhosa people of South Africa, was a Nobel Peace Prize winner in 1993 and became the first black President of South Africa in 1994. When he was put on trial in 1962 for leaving South Africa without the government's permission and for encouraging blacks to boycott work in non-violent protests against apartheid, he startled people by wearing the traditional dress, including a leopard-skin cape, of the native Xhosa people. 3) While serving time in prison for his role in protesting apartheid in South Africa, Nelson Mandela and the other black prisoners were forced to wear shorts, even in very cold weather, although white prisoners could wear long pants.[132]

• Swedish inventor Alfred Nobel performed experiments on dangerous materials in his Nobel Laboratory in Stockholm, Sweden. Unfortunately, an explosion involving nitroglycerin occurred in 1864, killing his youngest brother and several other people. Stockholm officials responded by banning experiments with nitroglycerin in the city, forcing Mr. Nobel to perform his experiments outside the city on a barge in the middle of a lake. Mr. Nobel became wealthy after inventing dynamite, but he felt guilty for having invented such a destructive substance, so he used his money to fund the Nobel Prizes, which are awarded annually in such categories as Peace, Literature, Chemistry, Physics, and Physiology or Medicine.[133]

Oceanographers

• Here are some oceanographer and ocean explorer stories: 1) One of the first scientific expeditions that Robert Ballard, the man who discovered the *Titanic*, was involved with used a sparker to map the ocean floor. The sparker set off explosions so that sound waves rebounded from the ocean floor. For three weeks, the explosions took place seven days a week, 24 hours a day, every 20 seconds. 2) Things deep in the sea are under tremendous pressure. Astronaut/ oceanographer Kathryn Sullivan owns a Styrofoam coffee cup that is the size of a thimble. It used to be regular sized until it was subjected to deep-sea pressure. 3) Eugenie Clark became interested in oceanography when she was a child. While her mother was working, she spent many hours looking at the fish in the old New York Aquarium. This introduction to oceanic life was much more conducive to creating an oceanographer than would have been watching the movie *Jaws*. 4) When Walter Munk decided to get a doctorate in oceanography in the early 1940s, his adviser told him that during the next ten years, he did not know of even one job in oceanography that would open up. Mr. Munk got his Ph.D. in oceanography anyway and became famous for his work using sound waves to measure the temperature of the oceans. [134]

Olympic Games

• Here's a trick question: How many gold medals were awarded at the first modern Olympic Games—the 1896 Games in Greece? The correct answer is zero. First-place winners were awarded silver medals, while second-place finishers were awarded bronze medals. By the way, the 1904 Olympic Games in St. Louis included some odd events, such as a tobacco-juice spitting contest.[135]

• The person behind the emergence of the Olympics as a modern-day sports competition was the Frenchman Baron Pierre de Coubertin. When he died, his body was buried in Lausanne, Switzerland, at the Bois de Vaux cemetery, but his heart was buried in Greece at Olympia.[136]

People with Handicaps

• Some great blues singers have been blind: 1) The life of blues singer Blind Willie Johnson was rough. When he was three, his mother died, and his father married another woman. When he was seven, his father discovered that this woman was cheating on him, so he beat her. She wanted to get revenge, so she threw lye water onto young Willie's face and blinded him. As an adult, Mr. Johnson got married and was respected as a gentle and dignified man, but in 1949 his house burned down, and he and his wife spent the night lying on wet mattresses. The next day, he went into the streets to earn money by playing his guitar and singing, but he caught pneumonia and died soon afterward. 2) Blues singer Sonny Terry became blind because of two accidents when he was a child. At age 11, he beat a stick against a chair, and a piece of wood broke off, flew up, and put out one of his eyes. When he was age 16, another boy threw a piece of metal at him and put out the other eye. 3) The great blues singer and guitarist Blind Lemon Jefferson received very little compensation for his recordings—he was often paid in full with a little money, a bottle of liquor, and a prostitute.[137]

• We have forgotten how much devastation the disease polio caused. In 1956, Tanaquil LeClercq, a George Balanchine dancer, contracted polio. It paralyzed her below the waist, and her dancing career and walking days were over at age 27. These days, we have a very effective vaccine for the prevention of polio.[138]

Politics and Politicians

• Here are some Madeleine Albright stories: 1) Big, important events sometimes conflict with everyday events. When Madeleine Albright learned that she would be named United States Secretary of State, she needed to fly out to Arkansas to meet with President Bill Clinton before the news of the appointment was made public. That meant that she had to call up everybody she had invited to a party and disinvite them. Fortunately, once the announcement that Ms. Albright would be the next Secretary of State was made, everybody understood why she had cancelled the party. 2) When Madeleine Albright was a member of the United Nations Security Council, she was the only woman among its 15 members. For Valentine's Day, she gave each of the men on the Security Council a bag of cookies, but since they weren't familiar with the American holiday, she had to explain what Valentine's Day was. 3) Madeleine Albright, United States Secretary of State under President Bill Clinton, got into politics early. She was campaigning for Democrat Adlai Stevenson even before she was a United States citizen. Ms. Albright was born in Czechoslovakia, and she became a U.S. citizen on August 14, 1957. 4) The press of Iraq once called United States Secretary of State Madeleine Albright a "serpent," so when Ms. Albright met a high-ranking Iraqi official, she made sure she was wearing a pin shaped like a snake. 5) Ms. Albright once said, "The solution to every problem begins with one person taking action." [139]

• Here are some Adlai Stevenson stories: 1) In the 1952 and 1956 Presidential elections, Adlai Stevenson ran unsuccessfully against General Dwight D. Eisenhower, a World War II hero. Once, Mr. Stevenson arrived late for a speech. He explained that he had been held up by a military parade, and then he added, "Military heroes are always getting in my way." 2) In 1952, Adlai Stevenson at first thought that he did not want to be a candidate for President, and he asked that his name not be brought up as a possible candidate. When Mr. Stevenson was asked what he would do if he were in fact nominated, he said, "I think I'd shoot myself." 3) After Adlai Stevenson was asked whether, when he was a boy, he had thought he might someday run for President of the United States, he replied, "Yes, but I just dismissed it as a normal risk that any red-blooded American boy has to take." 4) Adlai Stevenson once had Borden, his son, give a suit to a tailor to be repaired. The tailor looked at the suit, and then he told Borden, "Unless I'm mistaken, and I doubt that, this is the same suit I worked on for your father 15 years ago."[140]

• Here are some stories about politicians: 1) Republican Representative Craig Hosmer of California once made a rousing political speech during a campaign for re-election. Afterwards, a voter told him, "I like what you say, and I'll vote for you. Anything would be better than that Congressman we've got now." 2) Occasionally, the United States Senate gets in a mood to cut things. Once, Republican Senator Norris Cotton of New Hampshire was asked how the Senate felt about spending. He replied that if the 10 Commandments were introduced in a bill, the Senate would cut the bill down to 8 Commandments. 3) William D. Hathaway ran against Senator Margaret Chase Smith of Maine and won. During the campaign, he sent a telegram to Senator Smith—the telegram said, "I HOPE THAT THE BETTER MAN WINS."[141]

• Houston congressman Mickey Leland was a black politician who didn't mind shaking up white conservative Republicans. When he first arrived at the Texas legislature after being elected in the early 1970s, he wore an Afro and dashikis, and the establishment thought he was a Black Panther. Actually, they had something to be afraid of. He tried to pass a bill to help poor, old, ill people acquire relatively inexpensive generic drugs, but the drug companies and many doctors lobbied against the bill and succeeded in keeping it from being passed. After the vote dooming the bill, Mr. Leland walked up to several medical-association lobbyists and hissed at them, "You are evil motherf**kers!" He also succeeded in getting the bill passed in the next session.[142]

• Irish playwright Brendan Behan was much concerned with politics: 1) Mr. Behan was on an airplane trip when the air-flight attendant told the passengers, "We are coming into Dublin. Please tighten your belts." Mr. Behan yelled, "Let's leave politics out of this!" 2) A man sweeping the street outside the offices of the *Irish Press* saw Brendan Behan leaving the building and asked him who he thought would win the upcoming election. Mr. Behan replied, "Whoever gets in, you'll still be sweeping the street." 3) Brendan Behan knew a woman with two sons, about whom he said, "One of them is a politician; the other is an honest individual."[143]

• It hurts to lose a campaign for President of the United States. As columnist Mark Shields writes, "What it means for starters is that the first line of your obituary, '(fill in the blank), defeated presidential nominee, died yesterday at the age of,' has already been written." Walter "Fritz" Mondale lost a landslide election to Ronald Reagan in 1984, and George McGovern lost a landslide election to Richard Nixon in 1972. Mr. Mondale and Mr. McGovern met in 1988, and Mr. Mondale asked Mr. McGovern, "Please tell me, George, when does it stop hurting?" Although 16 years had passed since his loss, Mr. McGovern replied, "I'll let you know, Fritz. I'll let you know."[144]

• At a cabinet meeting during the Lyndon B. Johnson administration, several cabinet members complained that they didn't know what the American people wanted them to do. President Johnson asked, "And suppose we know what the people want us to do; can you be sure we ought to do it?"[145]

Popes

• While campaigning in the United States for John F. Kennedy, Irish playwright Brendan Behan was amazed to run across a group of Gaelic-speaking old ladies who were planning to vote for Richard Nixon. Mr. Behan wanted them to vote for Kennedy for President, so he asked them, "Did ye not hear what Nixon said about our holy Father the Pope?" The old ladies were shocked and wondered what Nixon had said, but fortunately the campaign truck drove off and Mr. Behan did not have to make something up to tell them.[146]

• Before Pope John XXIII received John F. and Jacqueline Kennedy, he enquired about the proper way to address the wife of the President of the United States and was told by the monsignor in charge of protocol to call her Madame President. However, when he met her, he simply opened his arms wide, smiled, and exclaimed, "Ah, Jacqueline!"[147]

• Several Cardinals once went to Rome as candidates for the Papacy. The only Cardinal who bought a return ticket home was the Cardinal who became Pope Pius X.[148]

Prayer

• Rabbi Levi Isaac of Berdychev once urged a tailor named Yankel to pray on the Day of Atonement. The tailor prayed, "I, Yankel, am a poor tailor who, the truth be told, have not been too honest in my work. I have occasionally kept remnants of cloth that have been left over, and I have occasionally missed the afternoon service. But Thou, O Lord, hast taken away infants from their mothers and mothers from their infants. Let us on this Day of Days be quits. Mayest Thou forgive me as I forgive Thee." After hearing the prayer, Rabbi Isaac said, "O Yankel, Yankel, why did you let God off so lightly!"[149]

• Here are two stories: 1) Moses' brother, Aaron, was a peacemaker. According to tradition, when a quarrel broke out between two people, Aaron would go to each person and say that the other person felt terribly about the quarrel and was begging for forgiveness. 2) As Jewish theologian Abraham Joshua Heschel walked with Martin Luther King in Selma, Alabama, he felt that "my feet were praying."[150]

Chapter 4: From Prejudice to Puns

Prejudice

• The great black dancer Bill Robinson, aka Mr. Bojangles, was aware of the prejudice that existed in the towns where he entertained. Each time he arrived in a new town, he went to the local police station and made friends with the police—and got a permit for his gun. He also immediately purchased a train ticket in case he had to get out of town quick. Only then would he go to his lodging and get ready for the show. In Pittsburgh, Pa., Mr. Robinson heard a white woman, Mrs. Annie Bies, scream. She pointed to a fleeing black youth who had stolen her pocketbook. Mr. Robinson took off after the youth and shot into the air with his pistol. A police officer, Michael Horan, arrived on the scene, and seeing a black man with a gun, opened fire and wounded Mr. Robinson in the arm. Later, Mr. Robinson was asked how he felt about being shot while trying to help a white woman. He replied that he was not angry at Officer Horan. His forgiving response to being wounded helped cement good relations with the police. Throughout his career, Mr. Bojangles worked to be on good terms with the law—for example, by holding benefits for the widows of police officers killed in action.[151]

• Sometimes, people of great moral courage are not treated well. During World War II, Jean Kowalyk Berger helped 14 Jews to survive by hiding them in the attic of her house in the Ukraine. Later, she emigrated to the United States, where she experienced great hardship. She went to the HIAS [Hebrew Immigrant Aid Society] to ask for help, but they told her, "I'm sorry to say, you know you are Christian, and we help only Jewish people." She replied, "You have the heart to say [that] to me, when I was expecting to be killed every moment with all my family, when the people during the night came to me and asked me to help them, to save their lives—I didn't tell them, 'Go away because you are Jewish.'" (Other Jews have treated her well. She is recognized as one of the Righteous, and in 1985, she was honored by Yad Vashem.) [152]

• In the late 1930s and early 1940s, Ralph Bunche and Gunnar Myrdal sometimes traveled together in the South. Mr. Myrdal was white, and so he could easily find a place to stay. Mr. Bunche, however, was black and because of Jim Crow laws, he often found it difficult to find a place to stay. Usually, he stayed with an African-American family in small towns, but once when the Ku Klux Klan was terrorizing the area, the only place he could find to stay was in an African-American mortuary. He slept on a slab, and on the slab next to him, separated from him by only a curtain, lay a corpse. In 1950, Mr. Bunche became the first African-American to win the Nobel Peace Prize.[153]

• When African-American Hall-of-Famer Frank Robinson was playing minor-league baseball in Columbia, South Carolina, he ran into a problem with three drunken home fans who hurled insults at him during a game. After a game, Mr. Robinson grabbed a baseball bat and started for the abusive fans, but fortunately the other African-American player on the team, Marv Williams, stopped him before he did major damage and perhaps ended up lynched. Manager Ernie White, a white man, investigated quickly and found out what the home fans had been saying to Mr. Robinson. The taunts made Mr. White furious. He ran after the three home fans, got their license plate number, and wrote the car's owner, saying that if the abusive home fans ever wished to meet Mr. Robinson and test his courage, he would set up a meeting. The three abusive home fans never set up the meeting and never returned to the ballpark.[154]

• Muhammad Ali is famous in part for saying, "Float like a butterfly; sting like a bee," but it was his friend Bundini Brown who coined the memorable words. Mr. Ali treated reporters well. He was always good for a quote during his boxing days, and he turned down few requests for interviews, including requests from reporters for high school newspapers. By the way, even after Cassius Clay (he later changed his name to Muhammad Ali) won an Olympic gold medal in 1960, he still couldn't get served in white restaurants in his hometown of Louisville, Kentucky. He went into a hamburger joint wearing his gold medal, but he wasn't allowed to eat there. According to some stories, young Cassius was so disgusted by how he was treated that he threw his gold medal into the Ohio River.[155]

• Segregation was a big part of the Broadway scene for many years. In 1932, the musical *Flying Colors*, which was choreographed by Agnes de Mille and Warren Leonard, became the first Broadway show to mix races. However, the dressing rooms and backstage areas were segregated. In addition, the black dancers were given the most dangerous jobs. In one number, the dancers were on ladders—the white dancers were on the bottom rungs of the ladder, which were safer, and the black dancers were seated at the top. During a performance, one ladder fell and like a stack of dominos, all the other ladders fell. One black woman had to be taken to the hospital—knowing that she was going to fall, she became hysterical, and her hands froze to the wooden rungs of the ladder.[156]

• Segregation was a problem all over America, not just in the South. In 1930, Agnes de Mille gave a performance at the Little Theater in New York for managers and agents. She filled the orchestra seats but roped off the balcony. Invited to attend the performance was her black cook-housekeeper, but the management of the theater wouldn't let her sit among the white managers and agents. They made her sit in the empty balcony—something that Ms. de Mille learned after her performance. In Hollywood in 1944, Agnes de Mille wanted to take black choreographer Katherine Dunham to lunch, so she went to Chasen's. Ms. de Mille, some friends, and Ms. Dunham and her husband were forced to eat alone in a huge upstairs banquet room, although there were several empty tables downstairs where the other customers ate.[157]

• African-American author James Baldwin was a victim of prejudice as he was growing up in New York City. When he was 13, he crossed the street to get to a public library on 42nd Street. A white police officer saw him and told him, "Why don't you n*ggers stay uptown where you belong?" Mr. Baldwin once met with Bobby Kennedy to plead for civil rights for his people. Mr. Kennedy told him that his Irish immigrant grandparents had been victims of prejudice but that now his brother was President of the United States. But Mr. Baldwin replied, "Your family has been here for three generations, and your brother's on top. My family has been here a lot longer than that, and we're on the bottom. That's the heart of the problem."[158]

• In 1961, Frank Robinson and Vada Pinson helped the Cincinnati Reds win the pennant—their first since 1940. Cincinnati fans were celebrating, and Mr. Robinson and Mr. Pinson, African Americans both, went to celebrate with their white teammates at a downtown club. Mr. Robinson and Mr. Pinson were refused admittance because of the color of their skin, but when the club's owner found out who they were, he made an exception to his policy and allowed them to enter the club. Mr. Robinson and Mr. Pinson walked in that door and immediately walked out the other door, then celebrated at a place where they knew they were welcome.[159]

• Some ways of fighting prejudice can be dangerous. In Pennsylvania's coal district, a black baseball team played a game that was umpired by a local sheriff who made it no secret that he was prejudiced. Fed up, catcher Louis Santop walked out to the pitcher's mound and requested that the pitcher throw a high, hard fastball. The pitcher did throw a high, hard fastball, and Mr. Santop made no effort to stop it. The high, hard fastball hit the prejudiced umpire in the neck, and suddenly the white fans in the stands were furious. The black ballplayers ran to their cars and fled, pursued for a few miles by furious white fans.[160]

• Shortly after Maya Angelou graduated from the eighth grade, she developed two very painful dental cavities. The town of Stamps, Arkansas, was segregated at the time, and the black dentist was far away. However, during the Great Depression Ms. Angelou's grandmother had lent money to the white dentist in Stamps, so she took young Maya there. However, the dentist said flatly, "My policy is I'd rather stick my hand in a dog's mouth than in a n*gger's." Nevertheless, Maya's grandmother was able to get $10 from him, and the money helped pay for the trip to the black dentist.[161]

• John Lewis, an African American who was active during the Civil Rights Movement, suffered from prejudice while growing up in Pike County, Alabama. He was the son of sharecroppers, and when he went to the library to get a library card, the librarian told him that the library was for white people only. The story has a happy ending. He marched and helped get civil rights for his people, and he was elected to Congress. As an adult author, he went back to that same library for a book signing—and he got a library card.[162]

• Early in her life, Marian Anderson went to a Philadelphia music school and asked to take lessons, but she was told, "We don't take colored." Refusing to give up, she took private lessons from soprano Mary Saunders Patterson and tenor Giuseppe Boghetti. Years later, maestro Arturo Toscanini heard her sing and told her, "Yours is a voice one hears once in a hundred years." When the movie *Young Mr. Lincoln* opened in Springfield, Illinois, Marian Anderson was invited to sing; however, she was turned away from the Lincoln Hotel because of the color of her skin. Several restaurants refused to serve her for the same reason.[163]

• The great dancer Bill Robinson, aka Mr. Bojangles, worked to overcome prejudice, but he was aware of the things he could not change. Once, he asked a white woman, Lillian Alpert Wolf, to choose some "girly" items he could buy at Nat Lewis' haberdashery as gifts. On the street, he started running ahead of Ms. Lewis. She called for him to stop running, as she couldn't keep up, but he shouted back at her, "You can't walk with me on Broadway. I'm a black man and you're a white lady. You meet me at Nat Lewis.'"[164]

• Jewish comedian Sid Caesar served honorably in the Marines and even ended up in a hospital bed for a while during his tour of duty. One day, two anti-Semite Marines came into the hospital to talk about "cowardly" Jews. One looked at Mr. Caesar's medical chart to find out his religion, then told the other Marine, "I told you this one was a yellow Jew." Mr. Caesar smashed a glass water pitcher, picked up a jagged shard, then held it against the Marine's throat and asked, "Now how yellow are these Jews?"[165]

• Some people of great moral courage are badly treated. During World War II, Mihael Michaelov helped many Jews in Bulgaria by keeping their property for them and by bringing them food. In addition, after the war he helped many Jews by giving them clothing and food. In 1969, he emigrated to Israel, but unfortunately, some Jews found out that he was Christian, so they put swastikas on his door and screamed "Goy! Goy! Goy!" at him. (Not all Jews were so prejudiced. In 1972, he was recognized as one of the Righteous by Yad Vashem.) [166]

• Lawyer Belva Lockwood wanted to argue a case in front of the U.S. Court of Claims in 1874, but Justice Drake refused to let her, saying, "Mistress Lockwood, you are a woman!" She fought in the courts and succeeded in getting a federal law passed that no one would "be excluded as attorney ... from any court of the United States on account of sex." As an attorney, she was very effective, winning a huge financial settlement for the Cherokee nation and sponsoring the first black Southern attorney to argue before the Supreme Court.[167]

• Zelma Watson George and her husband, Clayborne, a lawyer, fought racism. They lived in Cleveland, Ohio, and occasionally her husband would ask her, "Do you feel like fighting the race thing tonight?" Almost always, the answer was yes, and they would go to a restaurant that they knew would not serve black people. Because the Georges were black, the restaurant workers would refuse to serve them, and then the Georges would talk to the manager and gather the names of witnesses. Then Mr. George would file a lawsuit.[168]

• In February of 1998, Maine voters repealed a law that protected homosexuals from discrimination. Two days later, a gay psychiatrist named Charles Mitchell started on his usual early-morning jog, and he was brutally beaten and woke up in a hospital with a broken jaw, a broken cheekbone, and a fractured skull. The police chief investigating the crime said, "We don't think for one second this was a random attack."[169]

• Country comedian Jerry Clower grew up in the South at a time when white people thought they were better than black people. During the Civil Rights movement, he remembers seeing a black woman with a child who was begging her for water. The black woman started to let her small daughter drink from a water fountain, but a big white man told her, "That n*gger don't drink out of that fountain—move on."[170]

• As an African-American, Ralph Bunche suffered from prejudice while living in Washington D.C. For example, when the family pet died, the Bunche family went to a pet cemetery, but they were told that the pets of African-Americans had to be buried separately from the pets of white Americans. In 1950, Mr. Bunche became the first African-American to win the Nobel Peace Prize.[171]

• The Anti-Slavery Society of Peoria, Illinois, once brought in Frederick Douglass to speak, but none of its members offered him a room to stay in. Since no hotel would offer him a room in those Jim Crow days, he ended up walking the streets of the town to keep warm. [172]

• In 1937, blues singer Bessie Smith suffered a car accident that nearly severed her arm. According to record producer John Hammond, two ambulances drove by her simply because she was an African American. Ms. Smith died because of the accident.[173]

Presidents (USA)

• Here are some JFK stories: 1) Of course, John F. Kennedy came from a very wealthy family, and he worried that it might keep him from getting the votes of workers. In West Virginia, he met a coal miner who asked if it was true that Mr. Kennedy had never had to do a hard day's work outside of military service. Mr. Kennedy admitted that it was true, and the coal miner replied, "You haven't missed a thing." 2) John F. Kennedy became a war hero during World War II after he helped rescue several of his men after his ship, *PT 109*, was sunk. Asked how he had become a war hero, he said, "It was absolutely involuntary. They sank my boat." 3) As a Senator, John F. Kennedy spoke without using index cards at press conferences. As a new President, he became more formal and recited carefully prepared answers from index cards. Asked why he was using index cards and sticking so closely to the text printed on them, he replied, "Because I am not a textual deviant." 4) Harry Truman called a man an SOB whenever he thought the man deserved it. President John F. Kennedy once said after tangling with the former President, "I guess Truman will apologize for calling me an SOB, and I will apologize for being one."[174]

• Here are some George Washington stories: 1) Because of George Washington's fame, Mount Vernon began to be much visited. Because of the many visitors, Martha Washington worried about running out of wine for the family's use, so she ordered that the visitors be served rum instead of wine. 2) Alexander Hamilton served as George Washington's secretary, but he was often late to meetings, placing the blame on a malfunctioning watch. After Mr. Hamilton was late once too often, Mr. Washington told him, "Sir, you must provide yourself a new watch, or I a new Secretary." 3) George Washington once stood with his back to the fire, but as the fire was very hot, he moved away from it. A friend observed that a general ought to be able to stand fire, but Mr. Washington replied, "It does not look well for a general to receive fire behind." 4) J.P. Morgan's librarian, Belle da-Costa Greene, was alleged to have burned some of George Washington's letters that were in his collection. When asked why she had done that, she supposedly replied, "Why not? Mr. Morgan can afford it."[175]

• Here are some more George Washington stories: 1) In the winter of 1753, George Washington, who was then 21 years old, traveled to Ford Le Boeuf in Pennsylvania to take a message to the French commander. On the return home, he and Christopher Gist ran into trouble on the Allegheny River when their raft jerked suddenly, sending Mr. Washington into the icy water, Fortunately, the two men made it safely to an island in the middle of the river. That night, the cold weather froze the river's water, and the two men walked across the river to the shore. 2) George Washington was a courageous soldier. During a battle in the French and Indian War, Mr. Washington had two horses shot from under him and his coat was pierced by four bullets. 3) General George Washington and 11,000 troops spent the winter of 1777-1778 at Valley Forge, Pennsylvania. Of his men, 3,000 died of hunger, cold, illness, and suffering that winter. In the spring, there was good news—the French had decided to join the war on the side of the Americans.[176]

• Here are some Calvin Coolidge stories: 1) President Calvin Coolidge considered himself a fisherman, although he wore white gloves while fishing and the Secret Service put the bait on the hook as well as retrieved his catch. President Coolidge also had a strange idea about the ownership of fish. He once ordered the Secret Service to take trout away from a fisherman two miles from where President Coolidge was fishing. According to President Coolidge, the other fisherman's catch consisted of "*my* fish." 2) Following a speech, President Calvin Coolidge met a woman who gushed, "Mr. President, I was so anxious to hear your speech at the opening of Congress, I had to stand the *whole* 45 minutes." President Coolidge replied, "So did I." 3) President Calvin Coolidge once complained about the weather by saying, "Well, it's been hot here. I was sitting here the other night with a lady who fainted. Don't know whether it was the weather or the conversation." [177]

• President Abraham Lincoln, a tall man, and his wife, Mary Todd, a short woman, once appeared before a crowd. President Lincoln addressed the crowd, saying, "Here I am, and here is Mrs. Lincoln. That's the long and the short of it." Judge Kelly of Pennsylvania was also a tall man. When the two met, they shook hands, then they compared heights: Lincoln was 6-foot-4, and Judge Kelly was 6-foot-3. Judge Kelly then said, "Pennsylvania bows to Illinois. My dear man, for years my heart has been aching for a President that I could look up to, and I've at last found him."[178]

• A photo shows President Barack Obama bending over so that a small African-American boy can touch his hair. Jacob Philadelphia was the boy, and he said to the President, "I want to know if my hair is just like yours. President Obama replied, "Why don't you touch it and see for yourself?" Jacob was hesitant, but he touched the President's hair when Mr. Obama said to him, "Touch it, dude!" Then President Obama asked, "So, what do you think?" Jacob replied, "Yes, it does feel the same." Now this African-American boy knows that someone with hair like his can be (and has been) President of the United States.[179]

• Senator Benjamin F. Wade of Ohio once recommended that President Abraham Lincoln fire General Ulysses S. Grant, and Lincoln, as he so often did, said that he was reminded of a story. Senator Wade exploded with anger, saying, "It is with you, sir, all story, story! You are the father of every military blunder that has been made during the war. You are on the road to Hell, sir, with this government, by your obstinacy, and you are not a mile off this minute." On hearing that he was only a mile from Hell, President Lincoln said, "Senator, that is just about from here to the Capitol, is it not?" Senator Wade was not amused.[180]

• President Calvin Coolidge seldom spoke. At a dinner, a socialite was delighted to be seated next to him, but the President's wife, Grace, told her, "I'm sorry for you. You'll have to do all the talking yourself." He was also a teetotaler, but on one occasion, actress Marion Davies served him wine but told him it was fruit juice. President Coolidge drank three glasses and told Ms. Davies, "I don't know when I've had anything so refreshing."[181]

• Abraham Lincoln used to tell a story about a man who was attacked by a farmer's boar. The man grabbed a pitchfork and killed the boar. The farmer, however, was not pleased by the loss of a valuable animal, so he complained to the man, "Why didn't you use the blunt end of the pitchfork?" The man replied, "Why didn't the boar attack me with his blunt end?"[182]

• Franklin Delano Roosevelt once heard that people don't listen to the polite nothings that are uttered at social occasions. He chose to test this theory at a White House function where there was a long reception line. To each person he met, he said, under his breath, "I murdered my grandmother this morning." No one heard him, except for a Wall Street man, who replied, "She certainly had it coming."[183]

Problem-Solving

• Louisiana governor Huey Long wanted the vote of African-Americans, so he listened to African-American leaders. Once, some African-American leaders complained to him about a certain hospital where most of the patients were black, but none of the nurses were black. The African-American leaders wanted black nurses to get jobs there. Governor Long listened and said that he could get black nurses hired at the hospital, but that since he was governor of a state in which there was racism, the African-American leaders would not like his method. A few weeks later (and 35 years before the Civil Rights era), Governor Long visited the hospital in the company of several representatives of the media, and he pretended to be outraged, exploding, "It's a Gawd-damned disgrace! That hospital's full of n*ggers being tended by nice white girls! It's a Gawd-damned disgrace, and I won't stand for it!" Very quickly, the hospital hired black nurses.

Although Louisiana racists applauded his act and Louisiana liberals decried it, Governor Long had accomplished exactly the result the African-American leaders had wanted.[184]

• Mel Stone of the Chicago *Daily News* disliked it when other reporters lifted his articles, rewriting them and printing them in their newspapers. He once wrote about food riots in Serbia and mentioned a banner that said, "*Er us siht la Etsll iws nel lum cmeht.*" According to the *Daily News* article, this can be translated as "The municipality cannot aid." Jim and Dave McMullen lifted the article, rewriting it and publishing it in their *Post & Mail*, including the message on the banner. Mr. Stone gleefully pointed out that if you read the banner backwards, it says, "The McMullens will steal this sure." Later, he became general manager of the Associated Press of Illinois, for which he wrote an article about a rebel leader in India whose name was *Siht El Otspueht*. The United Press (which was not associated with United Press International) lifted the article, rewriting it and publishing it. Mr. Stone gleefully pointed out that if you read the rebel's name backwards, it says, "The UP stole this."[185]

• Ken Chenault was the Chair and CEO of American Express, and his father was a problem-solver. His father, Dr. Hortenius Chenault, was also a dentist, and in 1939 he made the highest score ever recorded when he passed the New York State dental licensing exam. He wanted to join the United States Army Dental Corps to help during World War II, but he was black, the U.S. Army was segregated, and he was not allowed to join the U.S. Army Dental Corps. Dr. Hortenius told his children much later, "No one was going to tell me what I could do." As a problem-solver, he did some research and he did some thinking and he learned French. He then joined the Allied Forces Dental Society, which was based in Europe and was not segregated. Ken says that he learned much from his father, lessons that he passes on to others: "As my father taught me, work hard, don't ever let anyone stop you or keep you down, focus on what you can control, and you can accomplish an extraordinary amount."[186]

• Other people had built steamboats before Robert Fulton, but Mr. Fulton showed that steamboats could be profitable modes of transportation. In 1810, Mr. Fulton had three steamboats carrying passengers and cargo in the Hudson and Raritan rivers. He had designed the steamboats so that they were double-ended. Because of this, they did not need to turn around in order to go back in the direction from which they came—the engine of a steamboat could make it go in either direction. Not everyone liked the steamboats designed by Robert Fulton. For example, fishermen worried that the contraption would scare fish away. During the early days of steamboats, sailing ships would sometimes try to disable them by ramming into their paddle wheels. Mr. Fulton was forced to make modifications to the design of his steamboats to defend against such attacks.[187]

• In the early 20th century, the white people of Australia decided to construct the Canning Stock Route to transport beef, which went from Sturt Creek in the north to Wiluna in the south—a total of 1,200 miles. To do that, the road would have to follow water sources across the desert. A man named Alfred Canning surveyed the route. Mr. Canning was a man of good problem-solving ability but a man of bad morality. He realized that the Aborigines knew where the water was, so he chained several Aborigines together. He also gave them no or very little water. Each day he released an Aborigine, and the Aborigine headed toward the nearest water source. Mr. Canning and his men followed the Aborigine and so learned the location of the water source. [188]

• In Washington, D.C., Sojourner Truth often took streetcars to get where she needed to go. However, because she was an African American, often the streetcars would not stop for her unless white people also were waiting for a ride. Once, several streetcars passed by her although she signaled for them to stop. Finally, Ms. Truth started shouting, louder and louder, "I want to ride! *I want to ride! I WANT TO RIDE!*" The elderly black woman attracted so much attention to herself that pedestrians stopped and traffic stopped—including a streetcar. Ms. Truth then quieted down and boarded the streetcar. Several passengers were amused at how she had tricked the streetcar driver into stopping.[189]

• General Zhi Bo wanted to attack a fortress in the mountains, but no road went to the fortress. Therefore, he ordered a huge bell to be built. When it was completed, he and his army departed, leaving the bell behind. The general of the mountain fortress saw the huge bell and desired it, so he ordered his soldiers to build a road so that the bell could be taken into the mountain fortress. A few days after the road had been built, General Zhi Bo returned and led his army up the road to the mountain fortress, which he quickly captured.[190]

• When Henry Ford first started manufacturing automobiles, they were a novelty. When he drove one in town, crowds of people gathered to look at it. Whenever he parked and went somewhere, then returned, he found someone in the driver's seat, trying to figure out how to make it run. To solve this problem, Mr. Ford began to chain his car to a lamppost whenever he had to leave it unattended for a few minutes. [191]

• During the Joseph McCarthy era, Hazel Wolf, a Canadian-born secretary in a law office and a former member of the Communist Party (when being a member was popular in America—the Depression) was arrested and thrown into jail because the government wanted to try her and get her deported back to Canada. However, she got out of jail by paying bail—and promising not to leave the country. (At age 100, Ms. Wolf was still in Seattle and was an active advocate for the environment.)[192]

• King Philip II of Macedon was sometimes opposed by powerful lords, but he came up with an original way of neutralizing their power. He simply went into the villages that supported a powerful lord and moved the villagers to a new village far away. In this way, he removed each lord's source of power.[193]

• Although they don't get much credit in the history books, washerwomen played an important role in the Crusades. The Crusaders wore heavy armor, didn't bathe often, and sweated a lot. The washerwomen made their lives less itchy by delousing them.[194]

Prohibition

• During Prohibition, many citizens detested the law that made alcohol illegal, and they declined to vote for anyone who wanted to enforce that particular law. A judge in Oklahoma, Robert L. Williams, once said it was impossible for a candidate for sheriff to be elected if the public knew that the candidate would enforce Prohibition if elected. Some sheriffs, however, did enforce Prohibition. During the Prohibition era, few sheriffs in the United States were women. An exception was Sheriff Laura Pratt of Macwahoe, Maine, who once received a report that a gang of rumrunners who had already eluded three sheriffs was coming toward her territory in a truck loaded with whiskey. Ms. Pratt headed toward a back road used by rumrunners, set up a roadblock, stood there armed with a rifle, and quietly made the arrests.[195]

• During the Prohibition era, William Johnson of Oklahoma earned the name "Pussyfoot" by sneaking up on stills and bootleggers in the middle of the night. He sometimes beat up bootleggers, and he admitted that to get convictions he frequently lied under oath in court. According to Pussyfoot Johnson, when it came to combating crime, "Ethics be hanged." This attitude was tolerated.[196]

Public Speaking

• Following the death of a good friend, James M. Barrie, author of *Peter Pan*, spoke at St. Andrew's University in Scotland. However, his speech started badly. He mumbled and the students could not hear him, and he played with a letter opener that he had absent-mindedly picked up. Suddenly, a student shouted, "Put it down, Jamie, or you'll cut your throat!" This roused Mr. Barrie, and he gave a good speech. Among other things he spoke of, he read to the students a letter that the explorer Robert Falcon Scott had written to him during his doomed South Pole expedition—the letter had been found on Mr. Scott's frozen corpse: "We are in a desperate state—feet frozen, etc., no fuel, and a long way from food, but it would do your heart good to be in our tent, to hear our songs and our cheery conversation."[197]

• While Calvin Coolidge was on the campaign trail, his train stopped at a small town. Coolidge stood briefly at the train's rear platform, looked the crowd over, and then he went back inside the train without speaking to the people by the railroad tracks. He explained to his friends inside the train, "This crowd is too big for an anecdote and too small for a speech."[198]

• Hugo Black once ran for the United States Senate. He started by making speeches in which he said that many people were asking him to run for the Senate, but he did not know whether he should. His wife asked him, "Hugo, who are all these people who keep wanting you to run for the U.S. Senate?" Her husband quietly replied, "Me."[199]

• Senator Hubert H. Humphrey loved to talk to the public—at great length. Senator Barry Goldwater once said that he had overheard a reporter say to another reporter during a Humphrey speech: "Trying to get anything out of this speech is like trying to get something out of *Playboy* magazine with your wife turning the pages."[200]

• Dwight David Eisenhower once was scheduled to speak at a dinner with three previous speakers who went well over their allotted time. Because of the lateness of the evening, when it was Mr. Eisenhower's turn to speak, he said that all speeches needed punctuation, and he was the period. Then he sat down. (It was a popular speech.)[201]

• Comic singer Anna Russell once went to the House of Lords, where she discovered that the Conservative politicians were all old men who slept through the speeches, while the Labour politicians were all young men who told each other jokes during the speeches.[202]

Puns

• When the American founding fathers signed the Declaration of Independence in 1776, they knew that they must band together in the war effort, for if Great Britain defeated the American colonies, they would be hanged. John Hancock advised his fellow signers, "There must be no pulling different ways; we must all hang together." Benjamin Franklin replied, "We must, indeed, all hang together, or most assuredly we shall all hang separately."[203]

• Gioacchino Rossini was once a guest of King George IV. Being polite, Rossini invited the King to sing while Rossini played. Although the King sang badly, Rossini tactfully continued to play. Afterward, when the King complimented Rossini on his tact, he answered, "Sire, it is my duty to accompany you—even to hell."[204]

Chapter 5: From Religion to Wit

Religion

• Tom Rath, a New Hampshire Republican, was a national counselor to Mitt Romney, 2012 candidate for President. (He was also one of Mitt's national counselors in 2008.) In the summer of 2010, Mr. Rath was arrested for driving under the influence with a blood-alcohol level of 0.11 percent. He offered to resign his position as one of Mitt's national counselors, but Mr. Romney told him, "No, you and I are joined at the hip." Then Mr. Romney, a Mormon whose religion approves of teetotalism, told Mr. Rath, a Catholic, "You know, Tom, if you belonged to my church, you wouldn't have had this problem."[205]

• The Bill of Rights recognizes that Americans have freedom of religion, but in the late 19th and early 20th centuries, the United States government banned Native American religions. Native Americans caught practicing such religious ceremonies as the Sun Dance could be imprisoned. Nevertheless, many Native Americans ignored the laws banning their religions and kept right on practicing them.[206]

• Famed skeptic Robert Ingersoll once proclaimed the death of the church, as he did not see in it any will to grow. But he had not considered the Methodists. Charles McCabe (later Bishop McCabe), who was working hard for the Methodists, sent this famous telegram to Mr. Ingersoll: "We're building two a day."[207]

Taxes

• The American colonists greatly resented a tax imposed on imported tea, and from being a favorite drink of the colonists, it became, in the words of Abigail Adams, "the weed of slavery." On December 16, 1773, under cover of the darkness of night, a band of colonists boarded some British ships in Boston harbor. Disguised as Native Americans, the colonists carried tomahawks and clubs, which they used to smash 342 chests of tea before dropping them into the water. In this Boston Tea Party, no one was hurt.[208]

• After Joan of Arc made history by freeing Orleans on April 28, 1429, and helped make Charles VII King of France, he asked what she wanted as a reward. She replied that she wanted the taxes lowered on her hometown of Domremy and on Greux.[209]

Telegrams and Telephones

• The President of the United States has the best telephone service imaginable. Joe Garagiola was once campaigning for and traveling with President Gerald Ford, and he was asked to call Johnny Bench about appearing with the President. Mr. Garagiola didn't have Mr. Bench's telephone number, but he picked up the telephone receiver, asked the White House operator to get him Johnny Bench, and before he could put the telephone receiver back in its cradle, Mr. Bench was on the other end of the line.[210]

• In the old days, telegrams almost always brought bad news. The parents of choreographer Léonide Massine once received a telegram telling them that their son Konstantin had been killed in a hunting accident. His mother read the message, stared at it, and then told the telegraph boy, "This isn't for us. You've made a mistake. Take it away." The telegraph boy assured her that there was no mistake, and she began to cry.[211]

• Alexander Graham Bell displayed his new invention—the telephone—at the Centennial Exhibition in 1876 in Philadelphia, Pennsylvania. Along with many other people, the Emperor of Brazil, Dom Pedro, wanted to try it. He picked the telephone up and held the receiver to his ear. When he heard a voice, he was shocked and dropped the telephone, exclaiming, "My God, it talks!"[212]

Theater

• The stagehands at Cambridge University took their Shakespeare seriously in 1934. During a performance of *Anthony and Cleopatra*, a drunk ran onto stage, disrupting the performance. Immediately, he was removed from the stage. After the play was over, the actors asked what had happened to the drunk, and a stagehand told them, "Don't worry—his trousers have been taken off." Punishment for disrespecters of Shakespeare was swift in those days.[213]

• In the old days, people felt that actors and actresses were immoral. The stage manager of the Benson Company, a traveling theatrical troupe, once inspected the dressing rooms of a small theater, and then picked out a room and said, "This one will do for the ladies." The local theater manager asked, "The ladies! Can't they dress with the gents? I thought the Benson Company was such a friendly one."[214]

• When Queen Victoria died, actor Lewis Waller started crying and said, "She's dead, she's dead!" He was inconsolable, and when a friend tried to advise him not to take her death so hard, he said, "It's the receipts—the receipts are bound to drop!" Just as he expected, they did.[215]

Titles

• Donald Trump's first book, *The Art of the Deal*, was a huge success, but unfortunately for him, when his second book, *Survival at the Top*, was ready to come out in paperback, Mr. Trump was in bankruptcy court and had been given an allowance to live on by his creditors. However, the paperback publisher avoided embarrassment by renaming Mr. Trump's second book, *The Art of Survival*.[216]

• William Burroughs' novel *Naked Lunch* received its title from novelist Jack Kerouac. According to Mr. Burroughs, "The title means exactly what the words say. NAKED lunch—a frozen moment when everyone sees what is on the end of every fork."[217]

Travel

• Early vaccinations sometimes left a scar. When Alicia Markova and other ballet dancers for the Ballet Russe de Monte Carlo received vaccinations before an international tour, they were given them in the leg. In Ms. Markova's case, this was a bad mistake, as her leg swelled up in a reaction to the vaccination. Fortunately, she recovered and went on to extend her international reputation. With Ballet Theatre, Alicia Markova toured several Latin American countries that were in the throes of revolution. While Ballet Theatre was in Bogota, Colombia, the British Embassy advised the dance troupe to stay in their hotel because "there is going to be shooting today." While touring with the Ballet Russe de Monte Carlo, Alicia Markova and the other dancers sometimes missed the luxury of baths. If they arrived early in a town, they used to go to a hotel, rent a room, and then give the maid a lot of money to bring them piles of towels. The dancers would then take 15-minute turns soaking in a bathtub filled with hot water until showtime.[218]

• African-American author Maya Angelou once traveled to Keta, Ghana, where she discovered a woman who strongly resembled her grandmother. Hundreds of years ago, slavers had come to Keta, where they had captured everyone except for some children who had run away. After the slavers left, the citizens of a nearby village cared for the now parentless children until they were grown up enough to rebuild Keta. Ms. Angelou strongly resembled the people now living in Keta, and they thought that she must be a descendant of the Keta people who were kidnapped and taken into slavery many years ago.[219]

• Prime Minister David Ben-Gurion often urged Jews to settle in Israel. Once an American Jew proudly told him that he had traveled to Israel nine times. Mr. Ben-Gurion exclaimed, "Nine times! Why don't you go just once?"[220]

Underground Jokes

• A citizen of the USSR died and went to Hell, where he noticed two signs. One pointed to Communist Hell; the other pointed to Capitalist Hell. The Soviet citizen began walking to Capitalist Hell. A devil saw him and said he was an idiot to go that way. The Soviet citizen protested that he had lived all his life in a Communist Hell—being tired of that, he now wanted to be in a Capitalist Hell. The devil then explained that in the Communist Hell when there was sulphur, there were no matches. And when there were both matches and sulphur, either the head devil was drunk and stayed away from work or the other devils were busy attending party meetings. In short, in Communist Hell, the fires were hardly ever burning. Meanwhile, in Capitalist Hell, because of the efficiency of the workers, the fires were kept roaring 24 hours a day.[221]

• Soviet Premier Nikita Khrushchev once met with President John F. Kennedy, and he asked how Kennedy came by his detailed knowledge of politics. President Kennedy explained that he got some of his information by calling Hell on his telephone, but that unfortunately the charge was $100 a minute. Back home in the Soviet Union, Premier Khrushchev decided to call Hell, but first he asked the telephone operator how much the cost would be. Surprised by the answer—a very low cost of five kopeks per minute—Premier Khrushchev asked why President Kennedy had to pay so much more than he. The telephone operator explained, "For President Kennedy, it's a long-distance call."[222]

• Adolf Hitler visited a fortune teller and asked when he would die. The fortune teller replied, "On a Jewish holiday." Hitler then asked, "Which one? Rosh Hashanah? Yom Kippur? Hanukkah?" The fortune teller replied, "Any day you die will be a Jewish holiday."[223]

Voters

• As a politician running for the office of President of the United States, John F. Kennedy shook many, many hands (sometimes using both of his hands), and his own hands were often sore. In addition, overeager fans reaching into his car sometimes tore off the buttons of his coat. Often, the cuffs of his shirts became shredded from his interactions with voters and fans, and so his aides carried around spare cuffs for him. Mr. Kennedy was not like some modern politicians who wished to avoid active service in the military. Mr. Kennedy tried to enlist twice in the United States armed forces during World War II, but he failed the physical examination both times. He used his family connections to get into the United States Navy, a branch of the armed forces in which he became a war hero.[224]

• Quite a few employees for Walt Disney played practical jokes. One of his animators captured some large horseflies that lived nearby because of the Disney stables. Knowing that Walt and his brother Roy were Republicans, the animators glued a little banner reading "VOTE FOR ROOSEVELT" to the horseflies' rear ends and let them loose in the Disney workplace near Roy's office.[225]

• Because the people of New Hampshire are not numerous and because they get involved in the Presidential election process so early, they have wonderful opportunities to meet the candidates. Back when Morris K. Udall was running for President, a reporter asked a resident of New Hampshire what she thought of Mr. Udall. She replied, "I don't know. I've met him only two or three times."[226]

War

• On September 1, 1983, during the Cold War, the USSR shot down Korean Air Lines Flight 007, killing all onboard, including US Congressman Lawrence Patton McDonald, from Georgia's 7th district. This led to heightened tension between the USSR and the United States. Shortly afterward, on September 26, Soviet army software engineer Stanislav Petrov was working at a surveillance center near Moscow. He remembered, "Suddenly the screen in front of me turned bright red. An alarm went off. It was piercing, loud enough to raise a dead man from his grave." What did the excitement mean? Mr. Petrov said, "The computer showed that the Americans had launched a nuclear strike against us." This first alarm was followed by a second alarm and then by a third alarm. He remembered that "for 15 seconds, we were in a state of shock. We needed to understand, what's next?" It was up to Mr. Petrov to make a decision: Was the United States really launching a nuclear attack against the Soviet Union, or was this a computer malfunction? He decided that it was a computer malfunction because the computer was saying that only five missiles had been launched against the USSR. He thought, *When people start a war, they don't start it with only five missiles. You can do little damage with just five missiles.* If Mr. Petrov had not made the right decision on September 26, 1983, the Soviet Union could have launched nuclear missiles against the USA, starting a nuclear war and perhaps ending the existence of civilization.[227]

• Funny and tragic and stupid incidents occurred during the Korean War. Captain Evelyn Decker, a U.S. Army nurse during the Korean War, remembers a funny incident involving one of two gay corpsmen she worked with who "were the best corpsmen we had." One of the corpsmen wanted to leave Korea and go back home, so he wrote the Pentagon to announce that he was gay. Captain Decker says, "The reply he received said he was doing such a great job that he had to stay." Tragically, Army nurses work on injured and dying soldiers. Captain Decker remembers that many of the newly injured soldiers who came into the medical facility where she worked were concerned about the condition of what they called their "family jewels." She remembers, "Not all were lucky enough to have their 'jewels' intact." Back in that racist time, some people, unfortunately, were stupid. Captain Decker remembers, "As some of the soldiers lay dying, they refused to let a black nurse [Captain Decker is African American] care for them. They'd rather die than be treated by a black nurse—and some of them did."[228]

• King Cao Cao decided to launch an attack against the state of Wuhuan although many of his officials advised against it. Despite many long and arduous difficulties, during which he had to kill thousands of battle horses to feed his soldiers, King Cao Cao conquered Wuhuan and then returned home. After his return, the King asked for a list of the officials who had advised him not to attack Wuhuan. The officials were afraid when King Cao Cao met with them, but he explained that their advice had been correct. True, he had won the war, but only after great difficulty. The best advice had been not to start the war at all. To encourage his officials to continue to give him their best advice, King Cao Cao rewarded them well with treasure.[229]

• Chips, a German shepherd/collie/huskie mix in the Army K-9 Corps, won both the Silver Star and the Purple Heart while fighting in Sicily, Italy, for General George Patton during World War II. Chips and the soldiers were pinned down on the beach when suddenly Chips ran toward and attacked the enemy soldiers in an Italian bunker. Enemy soldiers ran screaming out of the bunker, and the Allied soldiers saw Chips grabbing one enemy soldier by the throat. The remaining enemy soldiers surrendered. No problems occurred when Chips received the Silver Star and the Purple Heart, but when Chips met Supreme Allied Commander Dwight David Eisenhower, Chips bit his hand.[230]

• On May 10, 1775, Ethan Allen, Benedict Arnold, and their USAmerican soldiers captured the British fort Ticonderoga, located on Lake Champlain, New York. At dawn, they surprised the British. Mr. Allen ran up the steps to the quarters of the British officers, and there he met the British commander, who was still holding his pants in his hands. When the British commander asked in whose name Mr. Allen was demanding possession of the fort, he replied, "In the name of the great Jehovah and the Continental Congress." During the capture of Fort Ticonderoga, not one shot was fired.[231]

• Death due to friendly fire is not new. During the Civil War, Confederate General Thomas Jonathan "Stonewall" Jackson died at the hands of his own troops. At Chancellorsville, Virginia, he went scouting. Returning to his camp, he was mistaken by his own troops as the enemy. They shot General Jackson in the right hand and left arm, and the next day physicians amputated his left arm. Confederate General Robert E. Lee said after hearing the news, "He has lost his left arm, but I have lost my right." A few days after the amputation, General Jackson died from pneumonia.[232]

• House official Dong Anyu was an intelligent man who understood that in times of peace one must prepare for war. Sent to renovate a palace in a strategically located city, Dong Anyu ordered that tree trunks be used in the walls and that solid bronze be used for the pillars. Later, war started. The defenders of the city in which the palace stood began to run out of arrows, so they went to the palace and used the tree trunks to make arrow shafts and the bronze to make arrowheads. With their great supply of arrows, the defenders of the city were victorious.[233]

• During World War I, Sir Thomas Beecham was conducting Mozart's *Marriage of Figaro* at Drury Lane when an air-raid took place and bombs started falling and exploding. Sir Thomas thought that panicked audience members would be as much or more of a danger than the bombs, so he stayed calm and continued conducting despite the explosions coming from outside the theater. The audience members also stayed calm and stayed in their seats. The theater was not hit by bombs, and no one was injured.[234]

• Ethel Coffman, born 1895, remembered working in a fancy department store in Orange County, California, during World War II. The federal government regulated women's fashions to a large extent to save materials for the war effort. No cuffs or full skirts were allowed. The heels on women's shoes could be a maximum of one and a half inches. In addition, women were encouraged to donate their nylon stockings to the war effort so they could be recycled into such items as parachutes.[235]

• Near the end of the Civil War, Wilmer McLean gave permission for his house at Appomattox Court House, Virginia, to be the site where Confederate General Robert E. Lee surrendered to Union General Ulysses S. Grant. Following the surrender, Union officers wanted souvenirs, so they stole furniture from the parlor where the surrender occurred. Brigadier General George A. Custer, who was later killed by Native Americans at the Battle of Little Bighorn, stole a small table.[236]

• At the beginning of World War II, Anna Russell lived near some retired British colonels, many of whom booby trapped their property in case of invasion by the Germans. One colonel put electrical wiring all over his property. In case of invasion, he was prepared to throw a switch and electrocute the enemy. Another colonel had trenches dug in his property, and then he covered the trenches with plywood and sod, creating tank traps.[237]

• When Spike Milligan was drafted into the British armed forces during World War II, he showed up for a medical examination along with a lot of other draftees. A press photographer started to take a photograph of the mostly stripped draftees, but the recruiting Sergeant stopped him, saying, "For Christ's sake, don't! If the public saw a photo of this lot, they'd pack it in straight away."[238]

• World War I came very close to James M. Barrie, author of *Peter Pan*. He lost friends and loved ones in the war, and German planes dropped bombs so close to his home by the Thames River that on his balcony he occasionally found shrapnel. By the way, after James M. Barrie was named a literary baronet, he became Sir James M. Barrie, Bart. His wards often called him the Bart.[239]

• During World War II, Ballet Theatre asked Anton Dolin to stage *Pas de Quatre*. He wrote to Keith Lester to ask him to send over his notes on the ballet—using a notation developed especially for dance, the notes set down each step of the ballet. Unfortunately, War Customs refused to allow the notes to be sent, fearing that they were some kind of coded message.[240]

• *The Canterbury Tales* was being sung at the Metropolitan Opera on April 5, 1917, the day when the United States joined World War I. When news of the U.S.'s entry into the war spread throughout the Met, the opera was forgotten, and instead the orchestra played "The Star-Spangled Banner," which was followed by several cheers for the Allies.[241]

• Alexander the Great could be ruthless. When he was opposed by the Thebans, he conquered Thebes, killed at least 6,000 men, sold the Theban women and children into slavery, and destroyed all the buildings of the city except for its temples and the house of Pindar, a poet he greatly respected.[242]

• As a young recruit for the British armed forces during World War II, Spike Milligan was occasionally assigned to guard duty before going overseas to fight. However, he was not an intimidating guard. He used to say, "Halt! Who goes there?" But the other soldiers answered him by saying, "P*ss off."[243]

• During World War II, Adolf Hitler's German air force attacked London, England, with bombs, forcing citizens into bomb shelters for as long as 10 hours at a stretch. Making things even more difficult was that some bomb shelters didn't have bathrooms.[244]

• Nathan Rothschild was outspoken. Once a Major Martins was telling him about the horrors of war, and Mr. Rothschild interrupted with the comment that if many people had not died during wartime, presumably the major would still be a lieutenant.[245]

• During World War II, a touring company of Great Britain's Royal Ballet was almost captured when Adolf Hitler's Nazi Army invaded the Netherlands. The company escaped, but lost all its costumes, orchestral scores, and scenery.[246]

Weddings

• Here are some stories about Jackie and Caroline Kennedy: 1) When Jackie Bouvier married John F. Kennedy, she was supposed to be given away by her father, Jack Bouvier, but when she learned that he had been drinking, she declined to let him even come to the wedding. Stepping in at the last moment to give away the bride was Jackie's stepfather, Hugh D. Auchincloss. 2) In June of 1961, Jackie Kennedy, nee Bouvier, met Charles de Gaulle, President of France, and told him that her grandparents were French. President de Gaulle joked, "So were mine." 3) While living at the White House, young Caroline Kennedy used to ride a pony named Macaroni.[247]

• At traditional Jewish weddings, a glass is broken underfoot to remind the couple of the destruction of the Temple and to remind them of the suffering of the Jewish people in times past.[248]

Wit

• According to legend, when Robert Benchley and Dorothy Parker shared an office together at the Metropolitan Opera House, they had this sign painted on their door: "Utica Drop Forge & Tool Co. Robert Benchley, President. Dorothy Parker, President." Also according to legend, they applied to use this address for any cables sent to them: "Parkbench." (Mr. Benchley's son Nathaniel writes that they really didn't do these things, nor did Ms. Parker have the word "Men" painted on their door because she wanted people to drop by.) Other stories about Mr. Benchley include these: 1) Once, Mr. Benchley bought flowers at a florist shop named Waddly and Smythe. Leaving the shop, he said, "I wish I worked there. Then when people asked me what I did for a living, I could say, 'O, I waddly ... and I smythe." 2) Robert Benchley once signed a contract with David O. Selznick. Both parties were "parties of the first part," and the contract consisted of the words "I agree" above their names. 3) Mr. Benchley's politics are difficult to understand. He called himself a "confused liberal," and although he was a registered Republican, he usually voted Democratic. 4) Someone once told Robert Benchley that what he was drinking was "slow poison." Mr. Benchley replied, "So who's in a hurry?"[249]

• Here are some playwright/politician Richard Brinsley Sheridan stories: 1) Richard Brinsley Sheridan's father was an actor, something which didn't sit well with his classmates at Harrow. Because his father was an actor, Mr. Sheridan was insulted by the son of a physician. Mr. Sheridan defended himself by saying, "It is true my father lives by pleasing people, but yours lives by killing them." 2) Richard Brinsley Sheridan was once asked, "How is it that your name has not an 'O' prefixed to it? Your family is Irish, and no doubt illustrious." Mr. Sheridan, who was chronically in debt, replied, "No family has a better right to an 'O' than our family, for in truth we owe everybody." 3) Richard Brinsley Sheridan once met a couple of royal dukes, one of whom told him, "I say, we have been discussing whether you are a greater fool or rogue. What do you say?" Mr. Sheridan stood between the two dukes and then said, "Why, in faith, I believe I am between both." 4) Richard Brinsley Sheridan once got angry at Tom, his son, and he told him that he was going to leave him only a shilling in his will. Tom, who was always short of money, asked, "You don't happen to have the shilling about you now, sir, do you?"[250]

• Wit can make important social points: 1) During the Civil Rights era, people realized that racial relations were a matter of give and take. If white people weren't going to give black people their rights, the black people were going to take them. 2) Black people and white people in the United States had better learn to live together. The white people aren't going back to Europe, and the black people aren't going back to Africa. 3) Back in the Jim Crow days, a diplomat from Africa went into a southern hotel and asked for a room, only to be met with the reply, "We don't have rooms for your kind." The diplomat replied, "I don't want the room for me. I want it for my wife, and she is your kind." 4) A rabbi asked a black teenager if he was Jewish. The teenager replied, "Haven't I got enough trouble just being black?" 5) Black has always been fashionable in clothes, so why hasn't it always been fashionable in people?[251]

• In 1986, Fritz Hollings campaigned to be re-elected Senator from South Carolina. His opponent, a Republican who was fiercely anti-illegal drug, challenged him to take a test to see if he had been using illegal drugs. Senator Hollings replied, "I'll take a drug test if you take an IQ test."[252]

Appendix A: Bibliography

Aaseng, Nathan. *American Dinosaur Hunters*. Springfield, NJ: Enslow Publications, Inc., 1996.

Aaseng, Nathan. *The Inventors: Nobel Prizes in Chemistry, Physics, and Medicine*. Minneapolis, MN: Lerner Publications Company, 1988.

Aaseng, Nathan. *True Champions: Great Athletes and Their Off-the-Field Heroics*. New York: Walker and Company, 1993.

Adler, Bill. *Jewish Wit and Wisdom*. New York: Dell Publishing Co., Inc, 1969.

Alda, Frances. *Men, Women, and Tenors*. Boston, MA: Houghton Mifflin Company, 1937.

Aller, Susan Bivin. *J.M. Barrie: The Magic Behind Peter Pan*. Minneapolis, MN: Lerner Publications Company, 1994.

Anderson, Catherine Corley. *Jackie Kennedy Onassis: Woman of Courage*. Minneapolis, MN: Lerner Publications Company, 1995.

Anderson, Margaret J. *Isaac Newton: The Greatest Scientist of All Time*. Springfield, NJ: Enslow Publications, Inc. 1996.

Anderson, Margaret J., and Karen F. Stevenson. *Scientists of the Ancient World*. Berkeley Heights, NJ: Enslow Publications, Inc., 1999.

Bachelder, Louise, ed. *Abraham Lincoln: Wisdom and Wit*. Mount Vernon, New York: The Peter Pauper Press, 1965.

Beach, Scott. *Musicdotes*. Berkeley, CA: Ten Speed Press, 1977. Also: Peltz, Mary Ellis. *The Magic of the Opera: A Picture Memoir of the Metropolitan*. New York: Frederick A. Praeger, Inc., 1960.

Benson, Constance. *Mainly Players: Bensonian Memories*. London: Thornton Butterworth, Ltd., 1926.

Bernard, André. *Now All We Need is a Title: Famous Book Titles and How They Got That Way*. New York: W.W. Norton & Company, 1995.

Bernard, Catherine. *Sojourner Truth: Abolitionist and Women's Rights Activist*. Berkeley Heights, NJ: Enslow Publications, Inc., 2001.

Berry, Ralph, compiler and editor. *The Methuen Book of Shakespeare Anecdotes*. London: Methuen Drama, 1992.

Biggers, Don Hampton. *Buffalo Guns & Barbed Wire*. Lubbock, TX: Texas Tech University Press, 1991.

Block, Gay, and Malka Drucker. *Rescuers: Portraits of Moral Courage in the Holocaust*. New York: Holmes and Meier Publishers, Inc., 1992.

Block, Herbert. *Herblock: A Cartoonist's Life*. New York: Times Books, 1998.

Borge, Victor, and Robert Sherman. *My Favorite Intermissions*. Garden City, NY: Doubleday and Co., Inc., 1971.

Bryson, Bill. *The Mother Tongue: English & How It Got That Way*. New York: William Morrow and Company, Inc., 1990.

Butler, Jerry. *A Drawing in the Sand: A Story of African American Art*. Madison, WI: Zeno Press Children's Books, 1998.

Butz, Geneva M. *Christmas in All Seasons*. Cleveland, OH: United Church Press, 1995.

Camp, Carole Ann. *American Astronomers*. Springfield, NJ: Enslow Publications, Inc., 1996.

Camp, Carole Ann. *Sally Ride: First American Woman in Space*. Springfield, NJ: Enslow Publications, Inc., 1997.

Carter, Judy. *The Homo Handbook*. New York: Fireside Books, 1996.

Cheatham, Kae. *Dennis Banks: Native American Activist*. Springfield, NJ: Enslow Publications, Inc., 1997.

Clemens, Cyril, editor. *Mark Twain Anecdotes*. Webster Groves, MO: Mark Twain Society, 1929.

Clower, Jerry. *Ain't God Good!* Waco, TX: Word Books, Publisher, 1975.

Couric, Katie. *The Best Advice I Ever Got: Lessons from Extraordinary Lives*. New York: Random House, 2011.

de Mille, Agnes. *Portrait Gallery*. Boston, MA: Houghton Mifflin Company, 1990.

Decker, Captain Evelyn, U.S. Army. *Stella's Girl: The Autobiography of Captain Evelyn Decker, a World War II and Korean War Veteran*. New York: iUniverse, 2008.

Dickinson, Joan D. *Bill Gates: Billionaire Computer Genius*. Springfield, NJ: Enslow Publications, Inc., 1997.

Dole, Bob. *Great Political Wit*. New York: Doubleday, 1998.

Dole, Bob. *Great Presidential Wit*. New York: Scribner, 2001.

Dolin, Anton. *Alicia Markova: Her Life and Art*. New York: Hermitage House, 1953.

Eagling, Wayne; Robert Jude and Ross MacGibbon. *The Company We Keep*. London: Angus and Robertson, Publishers, 1981.

Epstein, Lawrence J. *The Haunted Smile: The Story of Jewish Comedians in America*. New York: PublicAffairs, 2001.

Epstein, Lawrence J. *Mixed Nuts: America's Love Affair with Comedy Teams From Burns and Allen to Belushi and Aykroyd*. New York: PublicAffairs, 2004.

Ewen, David. *Dictators of the Baton*. Chicago: Ziff-Davis Publishing Company, 1948.

Ewen, David, complier. *Listen to the Mocking Words*. New York: Arco Publishing Co., 1945.

Finck, Henry T. *Musical Laughs*. New York: Funk & Wagnalls Company, 1924.

Flammang, James M. *Robert Fulton: Inventor and Steamboat Builder*. Berkeley Heights, NJ: Enslow Publications, Inc., 1999.

Fesquet, Henri, collector. *Wit and Wisdom of Good Pope John*. Translated by Salvator Attanasio. New York: P.J. Kenedy & Sons, 1964.

Finlayson, Reggie. *Nelson Mandela*. Minneapolis, MN: Lerner Publications Company, 1999.

Fletcher, Lynne Yamaguchi. *The First Gay Pope and Other Records*. Boston, MA: Alyson Publications, Inc., 1992.

Fonteyn, Margot. *Autobiography*. New York: Alfred A. Knopf, 1976.

Ford, Michael Thomas. *The Voices of AIDS: Twelve Unforgettable People Talk About How AIDS has Changed Their Lives*. New York: Morrow Junior Books, 1995.

Foster, Leila Merrell. *Benjamin Franklin: Founding Father and Inventor*. Springfield, NJ: Enslow Publications, Inc., 1997.

Fradin, Dennis Brindell. *Washington's Birthday*. Hillside, NJ: Enslow Publications, Inc., 1990.

Garagiola, Joe. *It's Anybody's Ballgame*. New York: Jove Books, 1988.

Gardner, Robert, and Dennis Shortelle. *The Forgotten Players: The Story of Black Baseball in America*. New York: Walker and Company, 1993.

Garvey, Reverend Francis J. *Favorite Humor of Famous Americans*. Kandiyohi, Minnesota: Reverend Francis J. Garvey, 1981.

Gingras, Angele de T. *From Bussing to Bugging: The Best in Congressional Humor*. Washington, D.C.: Acropolis Books, Limited, 1973.

Gray, Bettyanne. *Manya's Story*. Minneapolis, MN: Lerner Publications Company, 1978.

Hanna, Edward; Henry Hicks; and Ted Koppel, compilers. *The Wit and Wisdom of Adlai Stevenson*. New York: Hawthorn Books, Inc., 1965.

Harmon, Ron L. *American Civil Rights Leaders*. Berkeley Heights, NJ: Enslow Publications, Inc., 2000.

Harris, Leon A. *The Fine Art of Political Wit*. New York: Dell Publishing Company, 1964.

Haskins, Jim. *Jokes from Black Folks*. Garden City, NY: Doubleday and Company, Inc., 1973.

Haskins, Jim, and N.R. Mitgang. *Mr. Bojangles: The Story of Bill Robinson*. New York: William Morrow and Company, Inc., 1988.

Hightower, Paul. *Galileo: Astronomer and Physicist*. Springfield, NJ: Enslow Publications, Inc., 1997.

Hintz, Martin. *Farewell, John Barleycorn: Prohibition in the United States*. Minneapolis, MN: Lerner Publications Company, 1996.

Hollihan, Kerrie Logan. *In the Fields and the Trenches: The Famous and the Forgotten on the Battlefields of World War I*. Chicago, Illinois: Chicago Review Press, 2016.

Howard, Megan. *Madeleine Albright*. Minneapolis, MN: Lerner Publications Company, 1999.

Hyman, Dick. *Potomac Wind and Wisdom: Jokes, Lies, and True Stories By and About America's Politics and Politicians*. Brattleboro, Vermont: The Stephen Greene Press, 1980.

Jacobson, Steve. *Carrying Jackie's Torch: The Players Who Integrated Baseball—and America*. Chicago, IL: Lawrence Hill Books, 2007.

Jones, Chuck. *Chuck Redux: Drawing from the Fun Side of Life*. New York: Warner Books, Inc. 1996.

Jones, Peter C., and Lisa MacDonald. *Hero Dogs: 100 True Stories of Daring Deeds*. Kansas City, MO: Andrews McMeel, 1997.

Karkar, Jack and Waltraud, compilers and editors. *... And They Danced On*. Wausau, WI: Aardvark Enterprises, 1989.

Kaufmann, Helen L. *Anecdotes of Music and Musicians*. New York: Grosset & Dunlap, Publishers, 1960.

Kent, Deborah. *The American Revolution: "Give Me Liberty, or Give Me Death."* Hillside, NJ: Enslow Publications, Inc., 1994.

Kent, Zachary. *The Civil War: "A House Divided."* Hillside, NJ: Enslow Publications, Inc., 1994.

Kolasky, John, collector and compiler. *Look, Comrade—The People are Laughing ....* Toronto, Ontario: Peter Martin Associates, Limited, 1972.

Kramer, Barbara. *John Glenn: A Space Biography*. Springfield, NJ: Enslow Publications, Inc., 1998.

Kristy, Davida. *Coubertin's Olympics: How the Games Began.* Minneapolis, MN: Lerner Publications Company, 1995.

Kristy, Davida. *George Balanchine: American Ballet Master.* Minneapolis, MN: Lerner Publications Company, 1996.

Ladré, Illaria Obidenna. *Illaria Obidenna Ladré: Memoirs of a Child of Theatre Street.* With Nancy Whyte. Seattle, WA: The Author, 1988.

Laskas, Jeanne Marie. *We Remember: Women Born at the Turn of the Century Tell the Stories of Their Lives.* Photographs by Lynn Johnson. New York: William Morrow and Company, 1999.

Lassieur, Allison. *Leonardo da Vinci and the Renaissance in World History.* Berkeley Heights, NJ: Enslow Publications, Inc., 2000.

Lazo, Caroline. *Alice Walker: Freedom Writer.* Minneapolis, MN: Lerner Publications Company, 2000.

León, Vicki. *Uppity Women of Medieval Times.* New York: MJF Books, 1997.

Lisandrelli, Elaine Slivinski. *Maya Angelou: More Than a Poet.* Berkeley Heights, NJ: Enslow Publications, Inc., 1996.

Litwin, Laura Baskes. *Benjamin Banneker: Astronomer and Mathematician.* Berkeley Heights, NJ: Enslow Publications, Inc., 1999.

Lyman, Darryl. *Holocaust Rescuers: Ten Stories of Courage.* Springfield, NJ: Enslow Publications, Inc., 1999.

Mackenzie, Richard. *A Wee Nip at the 19th Hole: A History of the St. Andrews Caddie.* Chelsea, MI: Sleeping Bear Press, 1997.

Markova, Alicia. *Markova Remembers.* Boston, MA: Little, Brown and Company, 1986.

Maser, Frederick E., and Robert Drew Simpson. *If Saddlebags Could Talk: Methodist Stories and Anecdotes.* Franklin, TN: Providence House Publishers, 1998.

Massine, Léonide. *My Life in Ballet.* Edited by Phyllis Hartnoll and Robert Rubens. London: Macmillan and Co., Ltd., 1968.

McCann, Sean, compiler. *The Wit of Brendan Behan*. London: Leslie Frewin Publishers, Ltd., 1968.

McCormick, Anita Louise. *The Industrial Revolution in American History*. Springfield, NJ: Enslow Publications, Inc., 1998.

McCormick, Anita Louise. *Native Americans and the Reservation in American History*. Springfield, NJ: Enslow Publications, Inc., 1996.

McPhaul, John J. *Deadlines and Moneyshines: The Fabled World of Chicago Journalism*. Englewood Cliffs, NJ: Prentice-Hall, Inc. 1962.

McPhee, Nancy. *The Book of Insults*. New York: St. Martin's Press, 1978.

Milligan, Spike. *Adolf Hitler: My Part in His Downfall*. London: Michael Joseph, Limited, 1971.

Mostel, Kate, and Madeline Gilford. *170 Years of Show Business*. With Jack Gilford and Zero Mostel. New York: Random House, 1978.

Muir, Robin. *The World's Most Photographed*. London: National Portrait Gallery, 2005.

Nachman, Gerald. *Seriously Funny: The Rebel Comedians of the 1950s and 1960s*. New York: Pantheon Books, 2003.

Nardo, Don. *Philip II and Alexander the Great Unify Greece in World History*. Berkeley Heights, NJ: Enslow Publications, Inc., 2000.

Nardo, Don. *The Trial of Joan of Arc*. San Diego, CA: Lucent Books, 1998.

Nichols, Richard. *A Story To Tell: Traditions of a Tlingit Community*. Minneapolis, MN: Lerner Publications Company, 1998.

Northrup, Mary. *American Computer Pioneers*. Springfield, NJ: Enslow Publications, Inc., 1998.

O'Brien, Steven. *Antonio López de Santa Anna*. New York: Chelsea House Publishers, 1992.

Parker, John F. *"If Elected, I Promise ...."* Garden City, NY: Doubleday & Co., Inc., 1960.

Peterson, T.F. *Nightwork: A History of Hacks and Pranks at MIT*. Cambridge, Massachusetts: MIT Press, 2011.

Pflaum, Rosalynd. *Marie Curie and Her Daughter Irene.* Minneapolis, MN: Lerner Publications Company, 1993.

Polking, Kirk. *Oceanographers and Explorers of the Sea.* Springfield, NJ: Enslow Publishers, Inc., 1999.

Poynter, Margaret. *Niels Bohr: Physicist and Humanitarian.* Berkeley Heights, NJ: Enslow Publishers, Inc., 2003.

Provenza, Paul, and Dan Dion. *¡Satiristas!: Comedians, Contrarians, Raconteurs & Vulgarians.* New York: HarperCollins Publishers, 2010.

Rabinowicz, Rabbi Dr. H. *A Guide to Hassidism.* New York: Thomas Yoseloff, 1960.

Radziwill, Lee. *Happy Times.* New York: Assouline, 2000.

Reynolds, Moira Davison. *Women Champions of Human Rights.* Jefferson, NC: McFarland and Company, Inc., 1991.

Rossi, Melissa. *Courtney Love: Queen of Noise.* New York: Pocket Books, 1996.

Rosten, Leo. *People I Have Loved, Known or Admired.* New York: McGraw-Hill Book Company, 1970.

Russell, Anna. *I'm Not Making This Up, You Know: The Autobiography of the Queen of Musical Parody.* New York: The Continuum Publishing Company, 1985.

Salkin, Jeffrey K. *Being God's Partner: How to Find the Hidden Link Between Spirituality and Your Work.* Woodstock, VT: Jewish Lights Publishing, 1994.

Schraff, Anne. *Ralph Bunche: Winner of the Nobel Peace Prize.* Berkeley Heights, NJ: Enslow Publications, Inc., 1999.

Schreiber, Penny and Joan Lowenstein, editors. *Remembering Raoul Wallenberg: The University of Michigan Celebrates Twentieth-Century Heroes.* Ann Arbor, MI: The University of Michigan Press, 2001.

Schulman, Arlene. *Muhammad Ali: Champion.* Minneapolis, MN: Lerner Publications Company, 1996.

Shawn, Ted. *One Thousand and One Night Stands*. With Gray Poole. New York: Da Capo Press, Inc., 1979.

Sheafer, Silvia Anne. *Aretha Franklin: Motown Superstar*. Springfield, NJ: Enslow Publications, Inc., 1996.

Slezak, Leo. *Song of Motley*. New York: Arno Press, 1977.

Slide, Anthony. *Eccentrics of Comedy*. Lanham, MD, and London: The Scarecrow Press, Inc., 1998.

Smith, H. Allen. *The Compleat Practical Joker*. Garden City, NY: Doubleday and Company, Inc., 1953.

Smith, H. Allen. *The Life and Legend of Gene Fowler*. New York: William Morrow and Co., 1977.

Smoot, Bill. *Conversations with Great Teachers*. Bloomington, IN: Indiana University Press, 2010.

Stanley, Phyllis M. *American Environmental Heroes*. Springfield, NJ: Enslow Publications, Inc., 1996.

Stephens, Autumn. *Feisty First Ladies and Other Unforgettable White House Women*. San Francisco, California: Viva Editions, 2009.

Stephens, Autumn. *Wild Women in the White House*. Berkeley, CA: Conari Press, 1997.

Story, Rosalyn M. *And So I Sing: African-American Divas of Opera and Concert*. New York: Warner Books, 1990.

Surge, Frank. *Singers of the Blues*. Minneapolis, MN: Lerner Publications Company, 1969.

Sutherland, Douglas. *The English Gentleman's Mistress*. London: Debrett's Peerage, Limited, 1980.

Swentzell, Rina. *Children of Clay: A Family of Pueblo Potters*. Minneapolis, MN: Lerner Publications Company, 1992.

Taylor, Peter Lane, and Christos Nicola. *The Secret of Priest's Ghotto: A Holocaust Survival Story*. Minneapolis, MN: Kar-Ben Publishing, 2007.

Tobias, Andrew. *The Best Little Boy in the World Grows Up*. New York: Random House, 1998.

Towle, Mike. *I Remember Sam Snead*. Nashville, TN: Cumberland House Publishing, Inc., 2003.

Udall, Morris K. *Too Funny to be President*. With Bob Neuman and Randy Udall. New York: Henry Holt and Company, 1988.

Verde, Tom. *Twentieth-Century Writers: 1950-1990*. New York: Facts on File, Inc. 1996.

Wagner-Martin, Linda. *Barbara Kingsolver*. Philadelphia, PA: Chelsea House Publishers, 2004.

Walker, Gerald, editor. *My Most Memorable Christmas*. New York: Pocket Books, Inc., 1963.

Warren, Roz, editor. *Women's Glibber: State-of-the-Art Women's Humor*. Freedom, CA: The Crossing Press, 1992.

Westman, Paul. *Neil Armstrong: Space Pioneer*. Minneapolis, MN: Lerner Publications Company, 1980.

Williams, John A., and Dennis A. Williams. *If I Stop I'll Die: The Comedy and Tragedy of Richard Pryor*. New York: Thunder's Mouth Press, 1991.

Wilson, Lori Lee. *The Salem Witch Trials*. Minneapolis, MN: Lerner Publications Company, 1997.

Wordsworth, R. D., compiler. *"Abe" Lincoln's Anecdotes and Stories*. Boston, MA: The Mutual Book Company, 1908.

Wukovits, John. *The Black Cowboys*. Philadelphia: Chelsea House Publishers, 1997.

Xuanming, Wang. *Six Strategies for War*. Singapore: Asiapac Books PTE LTD, 1993.

Xuanming, Wang. *Three Strategies of Huang Shi Gong*. Singapore: Asiapac Books PTE LTD, 1993.

Young, Robert. *A Personal Tour of Mesa Verde*. Minneapolis, MN: Lerner Publications Company, 1999.

Young, Robert. *A Personal Tour of Monticello*. Minneapolis, MN: Lerner Publications Company, 1999.

Yount, Lisa. *Antoine Lavoisier: Founder of Modern Chemistry.* Springfield, NJ: Enslow Publications, Inc., 1997.

Zall, P.M. *George Washington Laughing: Humorous Anecdotes by and about our first President from Original Sources.* Hamden, CT: Archon Books, 1989.

Zall, Paul M. *The Wit and Wisdom of the Founding Fathers.* Hopewell, New Jersey: The Ecco Press, 1996.

Zullo, Allan. *Escape: Children of the Holocaust.* New York: Scholastic, Inc., 2009.

Zullo, Allan, and Mara Bovsun. *Survivors.* New York: Scholastic, Inc., 2004.

Appendix B: About the Author

It was a dark and stormy night. Suddenly a cry rang out, and on a hot summer night in 1954, Josephine, wife of Carl Bruce, gave birth to a boy — me. Unfortunately, this young married couple allowed Reuben Saturday, Josephine's brother, to name their first-born. Reuben, aka "The Joker," decided that Bruce was a nice name, so he decided to name me Bruce Bruce. I have gone by my middle name — David — ever since.

Being named Bruce David Bruce hasn't been all bad. Bank tellers remember me very quickly, so I don't often have to show an ID. It can be fun in charades, also. When I was a counselor as a teenager at Camp Echoing Hills in Warsaw, Ohio, a fellow counselor gave the signs for "sounds like" and "two words," then she pointed to a bruise on her leg twice. Bruise Bruise? Oh yeah, Bruce Bruce is the answer!

Uncle Reuben, by the way, gave me a haircut when I was in kindergarten. He cut my hair short and shaved a small bald spot on the back of my head. My mother wouldn't let me go to school until the bald spot grew out again.

Of all my brothers and sisters (six in all), I am the only transplant to Athens, Ohio. I was born in Newark, Ohio, and have lived all around Southeastern Ohio. However, I moved to Athens to go to Ohio University and have never left.

At Ohio U, I never could make up my mind whether to major in English or Philosophy, so I got a bachelor's degree with a double major in both areas, then I added a master's degree in English and a master's degree in Philosophy.

Currently, and for a long time to come (I eat fruits and veggies), I am spending my retirement writing books such as *Nadia Comaneci: Perfect 10, The Funniest People in Dance, Homer's* Iliad: *A Retelling in Prose*, and *William Shakespeare's* Othello: *A Retelling in Prose.*

By the way, my sister Brenda Kennedy writes romances such as *A New Beginning* and *Shattered Dreams.*

Appendix C: Some Books by David Bruce

Anecdote Books

250 Anecdotes About Opera

250 Anecdotes About Religion

250 Anecdotes About Religion: Volume 2

The Coolest People in Art: 250 Anecdotes

The Coolest People in Books: 250 Anecdotes

The Coolest People in Comedy: 250 Anecdotes

Don't Fear the Reaper: 250 Anecdotes

The Funniest People in Art: 250 Anecdotes

The Funniest People in Books: 250 Anecdotes

The Funniest People in Books, Volume 2: 250 Anecdotes

The Funniest People in Books, Volume 3: 250 Anecdotes

The Funniest People in Comedy: 250 Anecdotes

The Funniest People in Dance: 250 Anecdotes

The Funniest People in Families: 250 Anecdotes

The Funniest People in Families, Volume 2: 250 Anecdotes

The Funniest People in Families, Volume 3: 250 Anecdotes

The Funniest People in Families, Volume 4: 250 Anecdotes

The Funniest People in Families, Volume 5: 250 Anecdotes

The Funniest People in Families, Volume 6: 250 Anecdotes

The Funniest People in Movies: 250 Anecdotes

The Funniest People in Music: 250 Anecdotes

The Funniest People in Music, Volume 2: 250 Anecdotes

The Funniest People in Music, Volume 3: 250 Anecdotes

The Funniest People in Neighborhoods: 250 Anecdotes

The Funniest People in Relationships: 250 Anecdotes

The Funniest People in Sports: 250 Anecdotes

The Funniest People in Sports, Volume 2: 250 Anecdotes

The Funniest People in Television and Radio: 250 Anecdotes
The Funniest People in Theater: 250 Anecdotes
The Funniest People Who Live Life: 250 Anecdotes
The Funniest People Who Live Life, Volume 2: 250 Anecdotes
The Kindest People Who Do Good Deeds, Volume 1: 250 Anecdotes
The Kindest People Who Do Good Deeds, Volume 2: 250 Anecdotes
Maximum Cool: 250 Anecdotes
The Most Interesting People in Movies: 250 Anecdotes
The Most Interesting People in Politics and History: 250 Anecdotes
The Most Interesting People in Politics and History, Volume 2: 250 Anecdotes
The Most Interesting People in Politics and History, Volume 3: 250 Anecdotes
The Most Interesting People in Religion: 250 Anecdotes
The Most Interesting People in Sports: 250 Anecdotes
The Most Interesting People Who Live Life: 250 Anecdotes
The Most Interesting People Who Live Life, Volume 2: 250 Anecdotes
Resist Psychic Death: 250 Anecdotes
Seize the Day: 250 Anecdotes and Stories

Children's Biography

Nadia Comaneci: Perfect Ten

Discussion Guides Series

Dante's Inferno: *A Discussion Guide*
Dante's Paradise: *A Discussion Guide*
Dante's Purgatory: *A Discussion Guide*
Forrest Carter's The Education of Little Tree: *A Discussion Guide*
Homer's Iliad: *A Discussion Guide*
Homer's Odyssey: *A Discussion Guide*
Jane Austen's Pride and Prejudice: *A Discussion Guide*
Jerry Spinelli's Maniac Magee: *A Discussion Guide*
Jerry Spinelli's Stargirl: *A Discussion Guide*
Jonathan Swift's "A Modest Proposal": A Discussion Guide

Lloyd Alexander's The Black Cauldron: *A Discussion Guide*

Lloyd Alexander's The Book of Three: *A Discussion Guide*

Lois Lowry's Number the Stars: *A Discussion Guide*

Mark Twain's Adventures of Huckleberry Finn: *A Discussion Guide*

Mark Twain's The Adventures of Tom Sawyer: *A Discussion Guide*

Mark Twain's A Connecticut Yankee in King Arthur's Court: *A Discussion Guide*

Mark Twain's The Prince and the Pauper: *A Discussion Guide*

Nancy Garden's Annie on My Mind: *A Discussion Guide*

Nicholas Sparks' A Walk to Remember: *A Discussion Guide*

Virgil's Aeneid: *A Discussion Guide*

Virgil's "The Fall of Troy": A Discussion Guide

Voltaire's Candide: *A Discussion Guide*

William Shakespeare's 1 Henry IV: *A Discussion Guide*

William Shakespeare's Macbeth: *A Discussion Guide*

William Shakespeare's A Midsummer Night's Dream: *A Discussion Guide*

William Shakespeare's Romeo and Juliet: *A Discussion Guide*

William Sleator's Oddballs: *A Discussion Guide*

(Oddballs is an excellent source for teaching how to write autobiographical essays/personal narratives.)

Retellings of a Classic Work of Literature

Arden of Faversham: *A Retelling*

Ben Jonson's The Alchemist: *A Retelling*

Ben Jonson's The Arraignment, or Poetaster: *A Retelling*

Ben Jonson's Bartholomew Fair: *A Retelling*

Ben Jonson's The Case is Altered: *A Retelling*

Ben Jonson's Catiline's Conspiracy: *A Retelling*

Ben Jonson's The Devil is an Ass: *A Retelling*

Ben Jonson's Epicene: *A Retelling*

Ben Jonson's Every Man in His Humor: *A Retelling*

Ben Jonson's Every Man Out of His Humor: *A Retelling*

Ben Jonson's The Fountain of Self-Love, or Cynthia's Revels: *A Retelling*

Ben Jonson's The Magnetic Lady, or Humors Reconciled: *A Retelling*

Ben Jonson's The New Inn, or The Light Heart: *A Retelling*

Ben Jonson's Sejanus' Fall: *A Retelling*

Ben Jonson's The Staple of News: *A Retelling*

Ben Jonson's A Tale of a Tub: *A Retelling*

Ben Jonson's Volpone, or the Fox: *A Retelling*

Christopher Marlowe's Complete Plays: Retellings

Christopher Marlowe's Dido, Queen of Carthage: *A Retelling*

Christopher Marlowe's Doctor Faustus: *Retellings of the 1604 A-Text and of the 1616 B-Text*

Christopher Marlowe's Edward II: *A Retelling*

Christopher Marlowe's The Massacre at Paris: *A Retelling*

Christopher Marlowe's The Rich Jew of Malta: *A Retelling*

Christopher Marlowe's Tamburlaine, Parts 1 and 2: *Retellings*

Dante's Divine Comedy: *A Retelling in Prose*

Dante's Inferno: *A Retelling in Prose*

Dante's Purgatory: *A Retelling in Prose*

Dante's Paradise: *A Retelling in Prose*

The Famous Victories of Henry V: *A Retelling*

From the Iliad *to the* Odyssey: *A Retelling in Prose of Quintus of Smyrna's* Posthomerica

George Chapman, Ben Jonson, and John Marston's Eastward Ho! *A Retelling*

George Peele's The Arraignment of Paris: *A Retelling*

George Peele's The Battle of Alcazar: *A Retelling*

George Peele's David and Bathsheba, and the Tragedy of Absalom: *A Retelling*

George Peele's Edward I: *A Retelling*

George Peele's The Old Wives' Tale: *A Retelling*

George-a-Greene: *A Retelling*

The History of King Leir: *A Retelling*

Homer's Iliad: *A Retelling in Prose*

Homer's Odyssey: *A Retelling in Prose*

J.W. Gent.'s The Valiant Scot: *A Retelling*

Jason and the Argonauts: A Retelling in Prose of Apollonius of Rhodes' Argonautica

John Ford: Eight Plays Translated into Modern English

John Ford's The Broken Heart: *A Retelling*

John Ford's The Fancies, Chaste and Noble: *A Retelling*

John Ford's The Lady's Trial: *A Retelling*

John Ford's The Lover's Melancholy: *A Retelling*

John Ford's Love's Sacrifice: *A Retelling*

John Ford's Perkin Warbeck: *A Retelling*

John Ford's The Queen: *A Retelling*

John Ford's 'Tis Pity She's a Whore: *A Retelling*

John Lyly's Campaspe: *A Retelling*

John Lyly's Endymion, The Man in the Moon: *A Retelling*

John Lyly's Galatea: *A Retelling*

John Lyly's Love's Metamorphosis: *A Retelling*

John Lyly's Midas: *A Retelling*

John Lyly's Mother Bombie: *A Retelling*

John Lyly's Sappho and Phao: *A Retelling*

John Lyly's The Woman in the Moon: *A Retelling*

John Webster's The White Devil: *A Retelling*

King Edward III: *A Retelling*

Mankind: *A Medieval Morality Play* (A Retelling)

Margaret Cavendish's The Unnatural Tragedy: *A Retelling*

The Merry Devil of Edmonton: *A Retelling*

The Summoning of Everyman: *A Medieval Morality Play* (A Retelling)

Robert Greene's Friar Bacon and Friar Bungay: *A Retelling*

The Taming of a Shrew: *A Retelling*

Tarlton's Jests: A Retelling

Thomas Middleton's A Chaste Maid in Cheapside: *A Retelling*

Thomas Middleton's Women Beware Women: *A Retelling*

Thomas Middleton and Thomas Dekker's The Roaring Girl: *A Retelling*

Thomas Middleton and William Rowley's The Changeling: *A Retelling*

The Trojan War and Its Aftermath: Four Ancient Epic Poems

Virgil's Aeneid: *A Retelling in Prose*

William Shakespeare's 5 Late Romances: Retellings in Prose

William Shakespeare's 10 Histories: Retellings in Prose

William Shakespeare's 11 Tragedies: Retellings in Prose

William Shakespeare's 12 Comedies: Retellings in Prose

William Shakespeare's 38 Plays: Retellings in Prose

William Shakespeare's 1 Henry IV, aka Henry IV, Part 1: *A Retelling in Prose*

William Shakespeare's 2 Henry IV, aka Henry IV, Part 2: *A Retelling in Prose*

William Shakespeare's 1 Henry VI, aka Henry VI, Part 1: *A Retelling in Prose*

William Shakespeare's 2 Henry VI, aka Henry VI, Part 2: *A Retelling in Prose*

William Shakespeare's 3 Henry VI, aka Henry VI, Part 3: *A Retelling in Prose*

William Shakespeare's All's Well that Ends Well: *A Retelling in Prose*

William Shakespeare's Antony and Cleopatra: *A Retelling in Prose*

William Shakespeare's As You Like It: *A Retelling in Prose*

William Shakespeare's The Comedy of Errors: *A Retelling in Prose*

William Shakespeare's Coriolanus: *A Retelling in Prose*

William Shakespeare's Cymbeline: *A Retelling in Prose*

William Shakespeare's Hamlet: *A Retelling in Prose*

William Shakespeare's Henry V: *A Retelling in Prose*

William Shakespeare's Henry VIII: *A Retelling in Prose*

William Shakespeare's Julius Caesar: *A Retelling in Prose*

William Shakespeare's King John: *A Retelling in Prose*

William Shakespeare's King Lear: *A Retelling in Prose*

William Shakespeare's Love's Labor's Lost: *A Retelling in Prose*

William Shakespeare's Macbeth: *A Retelling in Prose*

William Shakespeare's Measure for Measure: *A Retelling in Prose*

William Shakespeare's The Merchant of Venice: *A Retelling in Prose*

William Shakespeare's The Merry Wives of Windsor: *A Retelling in Prose*

William Shakespeare's A Midsummer Night's Dream: *A Retelling in Prose*

William Shakespeare's Much Ado About Nothing: *A Retelling in Prose*

William Shakespeare's Othello: *A Retelling in Prose*

William Shakespeare's Pericles, Prince of Tyre: *A Retelling in Prose*

William Shakespeare's Richard II: *A Retelling in Prose*

William Shakespeare's Richard III: *A Retelling in Prose*

William Shakespeare's Romeo and Juliet: *A Retelling in Prose*

William Shakespeare's The Taming of the Shrew: *A Retelling in Prose*

William Shakespeare's The Tempest: *A Retelling in Prose*

William Shakespeare's Timon of Athens: *A Retelling in Prose*

William Shakespeare's Titus Andronicus: *A Retelling in Prose*

William Shakespeare's Troilus and Cressida: *A Retelling in Prose*

William Shakespeare's Twelfth Night: *A Retelling in Prose*

William Shakespeare's The Two Gentlemen of Verona: *A Retelling in Prose*

William Shakespeare's The Two Noble Kinsmen: *A Retelling in Prose*

Appendix D: Some Books by Brenda Kennedy (My Sister)

The Forgotten Trilogy
    Book One: *Forgetting the Past*
    Book Two: *Living for Today*
    Book Three: *Seeking the Future*
The Learning to Live Trilogy
    Book One: *Learning to Live*
    Book Two: *Learning to Trust*
    Book Three: *Learning to Love*
The Starting Over Trilogy
    Book One: *A New Beginning*
    Book Two: *Saving Angel*
    Book Three: *Destined to Love*
The Freedom Trilogy
    Book One: *Shattered Dreams*
    Book Two: *Broken Lives*
    Book Three: *Mending Hearts*
The Fighting to Survive Trilogy
    Round One: *A Life Worth Fighting*
    Round Two: *Against the Odds*
    Round Three: *One Last Fight*
The Rose Farm Trilogy
    Book One: *Forever Country*
    Book Two: *Country Life*
    Book Three: *Country Love*
Books in the Seashell Island Stand-alone Series
    Book One: *Home on Seashell Island* (Free)
    Book Two: *Christmas on Seashell Island*
    Book Three: *Living on Seashell Island*
    Book Four: *Moving to Seashell Island*
    Book Five: *Returning to Seashell Island*
Books in the Pineapple Grove Cozy Murder Mystery Stand-alone Series
    Book One: *Murder Behind the Coffeehouse*
Books in the Montgomery Wine Stand-alone Series
    Book One: *A Place to Call Home*

Book Two: *In Search of Happiness*... coming soon

Stand-alone books in the "Another Round of Laughter Series" written by Brenda and some of her siblings: Carla Evans, Martha Farmer, Rosa Jones, and David Bruce.

Cupcakes Are Not a Diet Food (Free)

Kids Are Not Always Angels

Aging Is Not for Sissies

---

[1] Source: Jerry Butler, *A Drawing in the Sand: A Story of African American Art*, pp. 28-29, 44-46.

[2] Source: Lauren Kelley, "7 Ways Citizens Are Using Humor and Creativity to Protest Injustice." AlterNet. 25 March 2012 < https://www.alternet.org/2012/03/7_ways_citizens_are_using_humor_and_creativity_to_protest_injustice

>. Also: No Access Sex Strike. <http://www.noaccesssexstrike.org/>. Accessed 26 March 2012.

[3] Source: J. David Ake, "A Protester Handed President Barach Obama a Note ...." Paid to See. <http://paid2see.tumblr.com/post/13166029288/a-protester-handed-president-barack-obama-a-note>. Accessed 26 November 2011.

[4] Source: Brandon Voss, "Stirring the Pot." *The Advocate*. 7 August 2009 <http://www.advocate.com/exclusive_detail_ektid103913.asp>.

[5] Source: Arlene Schulman, *Muhammad Ali: Champion*, p. 46.

[6] Source: Autumn Stephens, *Wild Women in the White House*, pp. 131, 135.

[7] Source: Michael Thomas Ford, *The Voices of AIDS*, pp. 30-31.

[8] Source: Lynne Yamaguchi Fletcher, *The First Gay Pope and Other Records*, pp. 41-42.

[9] Source: Allison Lassieur, *Leonardo da Vinci and the Renaissance in World History*, pp. 52, 54, 112.

[10] Source: Richard Nichols, *A Story To Tell: Traditions of a Tlingit Community*, p. 29.

[11] Source: Robert Young, *A Personal Tour of Monticello*, p. 32, 49-50.

[12] Source: Allison Lassieur, *Leonardo da Vinci and the Renaissance in World History*, p. 57.

[13]Source: Carole Ann Camp, *Sally Ride: First American Woman in Space*, pp. 39, 51, 65.

[14]Source: Paul Westman, *Neil Armstrong: Space Pioneer*, pp. 14, 50.

[15]Source: Barbara Kramer, *John Glenn: A Space Biography*, p. 18.

[16]Source: Paul Hightower, *Galileo: Astronomer and Physicist*, pp. 49ff.

[17]Source: Laura Baskes Litwin, *Benjamin Banneker: Astronomer and Mathematician*, pp. . 35-36, 95, 97, 99.

[18]Source: Carole Ann Camp, *American Astronomers*, p. 18.

[19]Source: Carole Ann Camp, *American Astronomers*, p. 27.

[20]Source: J. Edward Evans, *Charles Darwin: Revolutionary Biologist*, pp. 20, 29, 86.

[21]Source: Dennis Brindell Fradin, *Washington's Birthday*, pp. 27, 29, 33-34.

[22] Source: Mark Shields, "Desperately Needed Now: Genuine Humor." Creators.com. 14 August 2010 <http://www.creators.com/liberal/mark-shields/desperately-needed-now-genuine-humor.html>.

[23]Source: Lisa Yount, *Antoine Lavoisier: Founder of Modern Chemistry*, pp. 51-52, 88, 99-100, 102.

[24] Source: Katie Couric, *The Best Advice I Ever Got: Lessons from Extraordinary Lives*, pp. 110-111.

[25] Source: Autumn Stephens, *Feisty First Ladies and Other Unforgettable White House Women*, pp. 62-63.

[26] Source: Paul Provenza and Dan Dion, *¡Satiristas!: Comedians, Contrarians, Raconteurs & Vulgarians*, p. 34.

[27]Source: Nathan Aaseng, *The Inventors: Nobel Prizes in Chemistry, Physics, and Medicine*, p. 70.

[28] Source: Gerald Walker, editor, *My Most Memorable Christmas*, pp. 52-55.

[29]Source: Geneva M. Butz, *Christmas in All Seasons*, p. ix.

[30]Source: Margaret J. Anderson, *Isaac Newton: The Greatest Scientist of All Time*, pp. 23, 25.

[31]Source: Ron L. Harmon, *American Civil Rights Leaders*, pp. 39, 42-45.

[32]Source: Joan D. Dickinson, *Bill Gates: Billionaire Computer Genius*, pp. 10-11, 30, 39, 50, 71.

[33] Source: Mary Northrup, *American Computer Pioneers*, pp. 62, 64.

[34] Source: Victor Borge and Robert Sherman, *My Favorite Intermissions*, pp. 17-18, 175.

[35] Source: Henry T. Finck, *Musical Laughs*, pp. 38-39.

[36] Source: Nancy McPhee, *The Book of Insults*, pp. 17, 20.

[37] Source: Melissa Rossi, *Courtney Love: Queen of Noise*, p. 54.

[38] Source: Roger Ebert, "Raising Free-Range Kids." *Roger Ebert's Journal.* 28 June 2009 <http://blogs.suntimes.com/ebert/2009/06/raising_free-range_kids.html >.

[39] Source: Alexander Provan, Review of *The Book of Dead Philosophers* by Simon Critchley. *The Nation.* 20 October 2009 <http://www.powells.com/review/2009_10_20.html >.

[40] Source: Lori Lee Wilson, *The Salem Witch Trials*, p. 41.

[41] Source: Don Nardo, *The Trial of Joan of Arc*, pp. 35-36.

[42] Source: Lawrence J. Epstein, *Mixed Nuts*, p. 32.

[43] Source: John Wukovits, *The Black Cowboys*, pp. 39, 43.

[44] Source: H. Allen Smith, *Life and Legend of Gene Fowler*, p. 256.

[45] Source: Douglas Sutherland, *The English Gentleman's Mistress*, p. 43.

[46] Source: Nathan Aaseng, *American Dinosaur Hunters*, p. 36.

[47] Source: Nathan Aaseng, *American Dinosaur Hunters*, p. 81.

[48] Source: Bill Smoot, *Conversations with Great Teachers*, p. 242.

[49] Source: Margaret Poynter, *Niels Bohr: Physicist and Humanitarian*, pp. 15-16.

[50] Source: Margaret Poynter, *Niels Bohr: Physicist and Humanitarian*, p. 27.

[51] Source: Leo Slezak, *Song of Motley*, p. 20.

[52] Source: John F. Parker, *"If Elected, I Promise ...."*, p. 109.

[53] Source: John F. Parker, *"If Elected, I Promise ...."*, pp. 62-63.

[54] Source: Herbert Block, *Herblock: A Cartoonist's Life*, pp. 9-10.

[55] Source: Lee Radziwill, *Happy Times*, p. 135.

[56] Source: Mary Ellis Peltz, *The Magic of the Opera*, p. 19. Also: Scott Beach, *Musicdotes*, pp. 78-79

[57]Source: Margaret J. Anderson, *Isaac Newton: The Greatest Scientist of All Time*, pp. 56-57.

[58] Source: Mark Shields, "You Can Choose Your Friends." Creators Syndicate. 25 June 2011 <http://www.creators.com/liberal/mark-shields/you-can-choose-your-friends.html>.

[59]Source: Illaria Obidenna Ladré, *Illaria Obidenna Ladré: Memoirs of a Child of Theatre Street*, p. 7.

[60] Source: Frederick E. Maser and Robert Drew Simpson, *If Saddlebags Could Talk*, pp. 40-41.

[61]Source: Margot Fonteyn, *Autobiography*, p. 191.

[62]Source: Bob Dole, *Great Political Wit*, p. 27.

[63]Source: Leila Merrell Foster, *Benjamin Franklin: Founding Father and Inventor*, pp. 27-28.

[64] Source: Gerald Nachman, *Seriously Funny*, pp. 52, 94. Also: John A Williams and Dennis A. Williams, *If I Stop, I'll Die*, p. 41.

[65]Source: Darryl Lyman, *Holocaust Rescuers: Ten Stories of Courage*, pp. 97ff.

[66] Source: David King Dunaway, "Foreword" to this book: Linda Wagner-Martin, *Barbara Kingsolver*, pp. xi-xii.

[67] Source: David Ewen, *Dictators of the Baton*, pp. 216-217.

[68] Source: T.F. Peterson, *Nightwork: A History of Hacks and Pranks at MIT*, pp. 126-127.

[69]Source: Kate Mostel and Madeline Gilford, *170 Years of Show Business*, p. 129.

[70]Source: Judy Carter, *The Homo Handbook*, pp. 146, 188.

[71]Source: Andrew Tobias, *The Best Little Boy in the World Grows Up*, pp. 116, 178.

[72]Source: Lynne Yamaguchi Fletcher, *The First Gay Pope and Other Records*, p. 19.

[73] Source: Mike Towle, *I Remember Sam Snead*, p. 150.

[74] Source: Mike Towle, *I Remember Sam Snead*, p. 106.

[75]Source: Richard Mackenzie, *A Wee Nip at the 19th Hole*, pp. 2, 6, 66, 71.

[76]Source: Joe Garagiola, *It's Anybody's Ballgame*, pp. 78, 105.

[77]Source: Richard Nichols, *A Story To Tell: Traditions of a Tlingit Community*, pp. 33-34.

[78] Source: Allan Zullo, *Escape: Children of the Holocaust*, pp. 151-179.

[79] Source: Nathan Aaseng, *True Champions: Great Athletes and Their Off-the-Field Heroics*, pp. 112-114.

[80]Source: Moira Davison Reynolds, *Women Champions of Human Rights*, p. 34.

[81]Source: Rabbi Dr. H. Rabinowicz, *A Guide to Hassidism*, pp. 65, 93, 97-98.

[82] Source: Lynn Fredricksen, "Holocaust survivor addresses SHA [Sacred Heart Academy] for Diversity Day." *Post-Chronicle* (Connecticut). 15 February 2012 <http://www.ctpostchronicle.com/articles/2012/02/15/life/ doc4f3bec5a470e9590026028.txt?viewmode=fullstory>.

[83] Source: Nathan Aaseng, *True Champions: Great Athletes and Their Off-the-Field Heroics*, pp. 114-117.

[84]Source: Stuart Jeffries. "Memories of the Holocaust: Harry Spiro." *The Guardian*. 27 January 2010 <http://www.guardian.co.uk/world/2010/jan/27/ holocaust-memorial-day-harry-spiro>.

[85] Source: Peter Lane Taylor and Christos Nicola, *The Secret of Priest's Ghotto: A Holocaust Survival Story*, all pages.

[86] Source: Allan Zullo and Mara Bovsun, *Survivors*, pp. 5-29.

[87]Source: Darryl Lyman, *Holocaust Rescuers: Ten Stories of Courage*, pp. 105, 113-114.

[88] Source: Allan Zullo, *Escape: Children of the Holocaust*, pp. 104-130.

[89]Source: Don Hampton Biggers, *Buffalo Guns & Barbed Wire*, pp. 31-32, 40-43.

[90]Source: Don Hampton Biggers, *Buffalo Guns & Barbed Wire*, pp. 37-38, 40.

[91]Source: Margot Fonteyn, *Autobiography*, pp. 230-231.

[92] Source: Steven O'Brien, *Antonio López de Santa Anna*, pp. 52-53, 56, 58.

[93] Source: Paul Provenza and Dan Dion, *¡Satiristas!: Comedians, Contrarians, Raconteurs & Vulgarians*, p. 254.

[94]Quoted from Louise Bachelder, ed., *Abraham Lincoln: Wisdom and Wit*, pp. 7, 29, 42, 44-45, 51.

[95]Source: Leon A. Harris, *The Fine Art of Political Wit*, pp. 103-104.

[96]Source: Jerry Clower, *Ain't God Good!*, p. 113.

[97]Source: Rosalynd Pflaum, *Marie Curie and Her Daughter Irene*, pp. 77, 79.

[98]Source: Catherine Bernard, *Sojourner Truth: Abolitionist and Women's Rights Activist*, pp. 12-13, 16, 18.

[99] Source: Bill Bryson, *The Mother Tongue*, p. 140.

[100]Source: Don Nardo, *The Trial of Joan of Arc*, pp. 40-41.

[101]Source: Lori Lee Wilson, *The Salem Witch Trials*, pp. 36, 58.

[102]Source: Rev. Francis J. Garvey, *Favorite Humor of Famous Americans*, p. 7.

[103]Source: H. Allen Smith, *The Compleat Practical Joker*, p. 282.

[104]Source: Paul M. Zall, *The Wit and Wisdom of the Founding Fathers*, pp. 7-8.

[105]Source: Rev. Francis J. Garvey, *Favorite Humor of Famous Americans*, p. 17.

[106]Source: Margaret J. Anderson and Karen F. Stevenson, *Scientists of the Ancient World*, pp. 45, 47.

[107]Source: Margaret J. Anderson and Karen F. Stevenson, *Scientists of the Ancient World*, p. 43.

[108] Source: John J. McPhaul, *Deadlines and Moneyshines: The Fabled World of Chicago Journalism*, pp. 10-11, 36, 243-244.

[109]Source: Kate Mostel and Madeline Gilford, *170 Years of Show Business*, p. 105.

[110]Source: Bob Dole, *Great Political Wit*, p. 29.

[111] Source: Lee Radziwill, *Happy Times*, pp. 11, 59, and unnumbered pages at end of volume.

[112]Source: Cyril Clemens, editor, *Mark Twain Anecdotes*, p. 21.

[113]Source: Jack and Waltraud Karkar, compilers and editors, ... *And They Danced On*, p. 53.

[114]Source: Ted Shawn, *One Thousand and One Night Stands*, p. 86.

[115]Source: Morris K. Udall, *Too Funny to be President*, p. 220.

[116]Source: Moira Davison Reynolds, *Women Champions of Human Rights*, p. 65.

[117]Source: Paul M. Zall, *The Wit and Wisdom of the Founding Fathers*, p. 52.

[118] Source: Marc Dion, "Sixty Percent of My Pay — Cutting the Fat." Creators Syndicate. 16 January 2012 <http://www.creators.com/liberal/marc-dion/sixty-percent-of-my-pay-cutting-the-fat.html>.

[119] Source: John Wukovits, *The Black Cowboys*, pp. 56-57.

[120] Source: Tim Teeman, "Gore Vidal: 'We'll have a dictatorship soon in the US.'" *The Times*. 30 September 2009 <http://women.timesonline.co.uk/tol/life_and_style/women/the_way_we_live/article6854221.ece>.

[121] Source: Frank Surge, *Singers of the Blues*, pp. 15, 39, 51-52.

[122] Source: Rosalyn M. Story, *And So I Sing: African-American Divas of Opera and Concert*, pp. 50, 69, 94, 133-134.

[123] Source: David Ewen, *Listen to the Mocking Words*, pp. 47-48.

[124] Source: Helen L. Kaufmann, *Anecdotes of Music and Musicians*, p. 218.

[125] Source: Frances Alda, *Men, Women, and Tenors*, p. 110.

[126] Source: Henry T. Finck, *Musical Laughs*, p. 81.

[127] Source: Ron L. Harmon, *American Civil Rights Leaders*, p. 30.

[128] Source: Caroline Lazo, *Alice Walker: Freedom Writer*, pp. 28-29.

[129] Source: Rina Swentzell, *Children of Clay: A Family of Pueblo Potters*, p. 17, 26, 34, 38.

[130] Source: Robert Young, *A Personal Tour of Mesa Verde*, pp. 19, 24.

[131] Source: Kae Cheatham, *Dennis Banks: Native American Activist*, p. 85.

[132] Source: Reggie Finlayson, *Nelson Mandela*, pp. 11-12, 22, 29, 82 88.

[133] Source: Nathan Aaseng, *The Inventors: Nobel Prizes in Chemistry, Physics, and Medicine*, pp. 7-8.

[134] Source: Kirk Polking, *Oceanographers and Explorers of the Sea*, pp. 55-56, 64, 96, 104.

[135] Source: Davida Kristy, *Coubertin's Olympics*, pp. 60, 86.

[136] Source: Davida Kristy, *Coubertin's Olympics*, p. 117.

[137] Source: Frank Surge, *Singers of the Blues*, p. 23, 32, 34, 61.

[138] Source: Davida Kristy, *George Balanchine: American Ballet Master*, p. 87.

[139] Source: Megan Howard, *Madeleine Albright*, pp. 43, 69, 75, 78, 114.

[140]Source: Edward Hanna, Henry Hicks, and Ted Koppel, compilers, *The Wit and Wisdom of Adlai Stevenson*, pp. 25, 42, 44, 88, 90.

[141]Source: Angele de T. Gingras, *From Bussing to Bugging*, pp. 72, 104-106.

[142]Source: Roz Warren, editor, *Women's Glibber*, p. 119. The short essay is by Molly Ivins.

[143]Source: Sean McCann, compiler, *The Wit of Brendan Behan*, pp. 88, 90-91.

[144] Source: Mark Shields, "A Little Slack for John McCain." Creators Syndicate. 28 August 2010 <http://www.creators.com/liberal/mark-shields/a-little-slack-for-john-mccain.html>.

[145]Source: Leo Rosten, *People I Have Loved, Known or Admired*, p. 20.

[146]Source: Sean McCann, compiler, *The Wit of Brendan Behan*, p. 91.

[147]Source: Henri Fesquet, collector, *Wit and Wisdom of Good Pope John*, p. 71.

[148] Source: Constance Benson, *Mainly Players*, p. 280.

[149]Source: Rabbi Dr. H. Rabinowicz, *A Guide to Hassidism*, p. 40.

[150]Source: Jeffrey K. Salkin, *Being God's Partner*, p. 55.

[151]Source: Jim Haskins and N.R. Mitgang, *Mr. Bojangles*, pp. 106, 197-198.

[152]Source: Gay Block and Malka Drucker, *Rescuers: Portraits of Moral Courage in the Holocaust*, p. 240.

[153]Source: Anne Schraff, *Ralph Bunche: Winner of the Nobel Peace Prize*, p. 45.

[154] Source: Steve Jacobson, *Carrying Jackie's Torch*, p. 142.

[155]Source: Arlene Schulman, *Muhammad Ali: Champion*, p. 28, 35, 55.

[156]Source: Agnes de Mille, *Portrait Gallery*, pp. 38-40.

[157]Source: Agnes de Mille, *Portrait Gallery*, pp. 45-46.

[158]Source: Tom Verde, *Twentieth-Century Writers: 1950-1990*, pp. 108, 117.

[159] Source: Steve Jacobson, *Carrying Jackie's Torch*, pp. 140-141.

[160] Source: Robert Gardner and Dennis Shortelle, *The Forgotten Players: The Story of Black Baseball in America*, pp. 79-80.

[161]Source: Elaine Slivinski Lisandrelli, *Maya Angelou: More Than a Poet*, pp. 34-35.

[162] Source: Schreiber, Penny and Joan Lowenstein, editors. *Remembering Raoul Wallenberg: The University of Michigan Celebrates Twentieth-Century Heroes*, pp. 42-43.

[163]Source: Rosalyn M. Story, *And So I Sing: African-American Divas of Opera and Concert*, pp. 43, 46, 48.

[164]Source: Jim Haskins and N.R. Mitgang, *Mr. Bojangles*, p. 195.

[165]Source: Lawrence J. Epstein, *The Haunted Smile*, p. 139.

[166]Source: Gay Block and Malka Drucker, *Rescuers: Portraits of Moral Courage in the Holocaust*, pp. 232, 234.

[167]Source: Autumn Stephens, *Wild Women in the White House*, p. 54.

[168] Source: Connie Schultz, "Time To Add Another Woman to Nation's Statuary Hall." Creators Syndicate. 20 December 2009 <http://www.creators.com/liberal/connie-schultz/time-to-add-another-woman-to-nation-s-statuary-hall-2009-12-20.html>.

[169]Source: Andrew Tobias, *The Best Little Boy in the World Grows Up*, p. 203.

[170]Source: Jerry Clower, *Ain't God Good!*, p. 66.

[171]Source: Anne Schraff, *Ralph Bunche: Winner of the Nobel Peace Prize*, pp. 71-72.

[172]Source: John A. Williams and Dennis A. Williams, *If I Stop I'll Die*, p. 15.

[173]Source: Silvia Anne Sheafer, Aretha Franklin: Motown Superstar, pp. 28-29.

[174]Source: Bob Dole, *Great Presidential Wit*, p. 78-79. 81-82.

[175]Source: P. M. Zall, *George Washington Laughing*, pp. xxi-xxii, 19, 35-26.

[176]Source: Dennis Brindell Fradin, *Washington's Birthday*, pp. 11-13, 16, 23-24.

[177]Source: Bob Dole, *Great Presidential Wit*, pp. 69, 72, 74.

[178]Source: R. D. Wordsworth, compiler, *"Abe" Lincoln's Anecdotes and Stories*, pp. 16, 67.

[179] Source: Jonathan Capehart[1], "Photo speaks volumes about Obama and race." *Washington Post*. 24 May 2012 <http://www.washingtonpost.com/blogs/post-partisan/post/photo-speaks-volumes-about-obama-and-race/2012/05/24/gJQA2T2lmU_blog.html>.

[180]Source: R. D. Wordsworth, compiler, *"Abe" Lincoln's Anecdotes and Stories*, p. 29.

---

1.   http://www.washingtonpost.com/jonathan-capehart/2011/02/24/AB1tR7I_page.html

[181] Source: Autumn Stephens, *Feisty First Ladies and Other Unforgettable White House Women*, pp. 77, 82.

[182] Source: Edward Hanna, Henry Hicks, and Ted Koppel, compilers, *The Wit and Wisdom of Adlai Stevenson*, p. 60.

[183] Source: H. Allen Smith, *The Compleat Practical Joker*, p. 235.

[184] Source: Leon A. Harris, *The Fine Art of Political Wit*, pp. 17-18.

[185] Source: John J. McPhaul, *Deadlines and Moneyshines: The Fabled World of Chicago Journalism*, pp. 74-75.

[186] Source: Katie Couric, *The Best Advice I Ever Got: Lessons from Extraordinary Lives*, pp. 60-61.

[187] Source: James M. Flammang, *Robert Fulton: Inventor and Steamboat Builder*, pp. 91, 94.

[188] Source: Germaine Greer, "Chained Aborigines helped make this cattle road. Can art now tell its story?[2]" *The Guardian*. 8 August 2010 <http://www.guardian.co.uk/artanddesign/2010/aug/08/germaine-greer-yiwarra-kuju>.

[189] Source: Catherine Bernard, *Sojourner Truth: Abolitionist and Women's Rights Activist*, pp. 87-88.

[190] Source: Wang Xuanming, *Six Strategies for War*, pp. 141-143.

[191] Source: Anita Louise McCormick, *The Industrial Revolution in American History*, p. 102.

[192] Source: Jeanne Marie Laskas, *We Remember*, pp. 99-100.

[193] Source: Don Nardo, *Philip II and Alexander the Great Unify Greece in World History*, p. 42.

[194] Source: Vicki León, *Uppity Women of Medieval Times*, p. 124.

[195] Source: Martin Hintz, *Farewell, John Barleycorn: Prohibition in the United States*, pp. 62, 68.

[196] Source: Martin Hintz, *Farewell, John Barleycorn: Prohibition in the United States*, p. 65.

[197] Source: Susan Bivin Aller, *J.M. Barrie: The Magic Behind Peter Pan*, pp. 113-114.

[198] Source: Dick Hyman, *Potomac Wind and Wisdom*, pp. 14-15.

---

2.   http://www.guardian.co.uk/artanddesign/2010/aug/08/germaine-greer-yiwarra-kuju

[199] Source: Herbert Block, *Herblock: A Cartoonist's Life*, pp. 119-120.

[200] Source: Dick Hyman, *Potomac Wind and Wisdom*, pp. 17-19.

[201] Source: Bob Dole, *Great Presidential Wit*, p. 160.

[202] Source: Anna Russell, *I'm Not Making This Up, You Know*, p. 199.

[203] Source: Leila Merrell Foster, *Benjamin Franklin: Founding Father and Inventor*, p. 5.

[204] Source: David Ewen, *Listen to the Mocking Words*, p. 121.

[205] Source: Mark Shield, "Tolerant Americans 2012." Creators Syndicate. 14 January 2012 <http://www.creators.com/liberal/mark-shields/tolerant-americans-2012-12-01-14.html>.

[206] Source: Anita Louise McCormick, *Native Americans and the Reservation in American History*, pp. 91-93.

[207] Source: Frederick E. Maser and Robert Drew Simpson, *If Saddlebags Could Talk*, p. 80.

[208] Source: Deborah Kent, *The American Revolution: "Give Me Liberty, or Give Me Death,"* pp. 28, 31- 33.

[209] Source: Vicki León, *Uppity Women of Medieval Times*, p. 136.

[210] Source: Joe Garagiola, *It's Anybody's Ballgame*, p. 127.

[211] Source: Léonide Massine, *My Life in Ballet*, pp. 32-33.

[212] Source: Anita Louise McCormick, *The Industrial Revolution in American History*, p. 9.

[213] Source: Ralph Berry, compiler and editor, *The Methuen Book of Shakespeare Anecdotes*, pp. 141-142.

[214] Source: Constance Benson, *Mainly Players*, p. 42.

[215] Source: Ralph Berry, compiler and editor, *The Methuen Book of Shakespeare Anecdotes*, p. 106.

[216] Source: André Bernard, *Now All We Need is a Title*, pp. 86-87.

[217] Source: André Bernard, *Now All We Need is a Title*, p. 25.

[218] Source: Alicia Markova, *Markova Remembers*, pp. 80, 86, 120.

[219] Source: Elaine Slivinski Lisandrelli, *Maya Angelou: More Than a Poet*, pp. 90-92.

[220] Source: Bill Adler, *Jewish Wit and Wisdom*, p. 101.

[221]Source: John Kolasky, collector and compiler, *Look, Comrade—The People are Laughing ...*, pp. 128-129.

[222]Source: John Kolasky, collector and compiler, *Look, Comrade—The People are Laughing ...*, p. 119.

[223]Source: Lawrence J. Epstein, *The Haunted Smile*, pp. 123-124.

[224] Source: Robin Muir, *The World's Most Photographed*, pp. 92, 95.

[225] Source: Chuck Jones, *Chuck Redux: Drawing from the Fun Side of Life*, pp. 95-96.

[226]Source: Morris K. Udall, *Too Funny to be President*, p. 22.

[227] Source: Allan Little, "How I stopped nuclear war." BBC News. 21 October 1998 <http://news.bbc.co.uk/2/hi/europe/198173.stm>. Also: "Larry McDonald." Wikipedia. <http://en.wikipedia.org/wiki/Larry_McDonald>. Accessed 8 December 2010. Also: David Hoffman , "I Had A Funny Feeling in My Gut." *Washington Post*. 10 February 1999. <http://www.washingtonpost.com/wp-srv/inatl/longterm/coldwar/shatter021099b.htm>.

[228] Source: Captain Evelyn Decker, U.S. Army, *Stella's Girl: The Autobiography of Captain Evelyn Decker, a World War II and Korean War Veteran*. New York: iUniverse, 2008.

[229] Source: Wang Xuanming, *Three Strategies of Huang Shi Gong*, pp. 50-53.

[230] Source: Peter C. Jones and Lisa MacDonald *Hero Dogs: 100 True Stories of Daring Deeds*, pp. 172-173.

[231]Source: Deborah Kent, *The American Revolution: "Give Me Liberty, or Give Me Death,"* pp. 37-38.

[232]Source: Zachary Kent, *The Civil War: "A House Divided,"* pp. 57, 59-60.

[233]Source: Wang Xuanming, *Six Strategies for War*, pp. 132-136.

[234]Source: David Ewen, *Dictators of the Baton*, p. 224.

[235]Source: Jeanne Marie Laskas, *We Remember*, p. 65.

[236]Source: Zachary Kent, *The Civil War: "A House Divided,"* p. 108.

[237]Source: Anna Russell, *I'm Not Making This Up, You Know*, p. 88.

[238]Source: Spike Milligan, *Adolf Hitler: My Part in His Downfall*, p. 26.

[239]Source: Susan Bivin Aller, J.M. Barrie: The Magic Behind Peter Pan, pp. 102-103.

[240]Source: Anton Dolin, *Alicia Markova: Her Life and Art*, p. 254.

[241]Source: Frances Alda, *Men, Women, and Tenors*, pp. 226-227.

[242]Source: Don Nardo, *Philip II and Alexander the Great Unify Greece in World History*, p. 85.

[243] Source: Spike Milligan, *Adolf Hitler: My Part in His Downfall*, p. 31.

[244]Source: Megan Howard, *Madeleine Albright*, p. 20.

[245]Source: Bill Adler, *Jewish Wit and Wisdom*, pp. 18-19.

[246]Source: Wayne Eagling, Robert Jude, and Ross MacGibbon, *The Company We Keep*, p. 8.

[247]Source: Catherine Corley Anderson, *Jackie Kennedy Onassis: Woman of Courage*, pp. 29, 56-57.

[248]Source: Bettyanne Gray, *Manya's Story*, p. 52.

[249]Source: Nathaniel Benchley, *Robert Benchley*, pp. 3, 7, 16, 145, 193.

[250]Source: Leon A. Harris, *The Fine Art of Political Wit*, pp. 21, 33, 37, 39.

[251]Source: Jim Haskins, *Jokes from Black Folks*, pp. 46, 67, 71, 74, 94.

[252] Source: Mark Shields, "A South Carolina Giant." Creators Syndicate. 21 January 2012 <http://www.creators.com/liberal/mark-shields/a-south-carolina-giant.html>.